YESHIVA DAYS

Yeshiva Days

LEARNING ON THE LOWER EAST SIDE

JONATHAN BOYARIN

PRINCETON UNIVERSITY PRESS

PRINCETON *AND* OXFORD

Published by Princeton University Press
41 William Street, Princeton, New Jersey 08540
6 Oxford Street, Woodstock, Oxfordshire OX20 1TR

press.princeton.edu

Library of Congress Cataloging-in-Publication Data

Names: Boyarin, Jonathan, author.
Title: Yeshiva days : learning on the Lower East Side / Jonathan Boyarin.
Description: Princeton : Princeton University Press, 2020. | Includes
   bibliographical references and index.
Identifiers: LCCN 2020014813 (print) | LCCN 2020014814 (ebook) |
   ISBN 9780691203997 (paperback) | ISBN 9780691203980
   (hardcover) | ISBN 9780691207698 (epub)
Subjects: LCSH: Boyarin, Jonathan. | Jewish men—New York
   (State)—New York—Biography. | Mesivtha Tifereth Jerusalem
   (New York, N.Y.) | Yeshivas—New York (State)—New York. |
   Lower East Side, (New York, N.Y.)
Classification: LCC E184.37.B69 A3 2020 (print) | LCC E184.37.B69
   (ebook) | DDC 974.7/1092 [B]—dc23
LC record available at https://lccn.loc.gov/2020014813
LC ebook record available at https://lccn.loc.gov/2020014814

British Library Cataloging-in-Publication Data is available

Editorial: Fred Appel and Jenny Tan
Production Editorial: Leslie Grundfest
Jacket/Cover Design: Pamela Schnitter
Production: Brigid Ackerman
Publicity: Kate Hensley and Kathryn Stevens (UK)
Copyeditor: Aviva Arad

Jacket/Cover Credit: Old copy of the Talmud in a classroom at the
Lubavitch headquarters in Crown Heights, Brooklyn / Ira Berger / Alamy

This book has been composed in Arno

Printed on acid-free paper. ∞

Printed in the United States of America

10 9 8 7 6 5 4 3 2 1

To the memory of the Jews of Telz in Lithuania, members of the yeshiva and townspeople, martyred at the hands of the Nazis and their local collaborators.

CONTENTS

In effect, every project of ethnography enters sites of fieldwork through a zone of collateral counterpart knowledge that it cannot ignore in finding its way to the preferred scenes of ordinary everyday life with which it is traditionally comfortable. The fundamental problem here is in confronting the politics of knowledge that any project of fieldwork involves and the ethnographer's efforts to make this politics of knowledge itself part of the design of investigation.

—DOUGLAS R. HOLMES & GEORGE E. MARCUS,
"PARA-ETHNOGRAPHY" *HTTP://KNOWLEDGE.*
SAGEPUB.COM/VIEW/RESEARCH/N307.XML

The secret things belong to the Lord our God; but the things that are revealed belong unto us and to our children forever, that we may do all the words of this law.

—DEUTERONOMY 29:28

FOR CENTURIES, the central institution of traditional rabbinic learning among east European Jews and their descendants has been the yeshiva. The institution took its modern form in Lithuania and nearby portions of the Pale of Settlement over the course of the nineteenth century, as a place dedicated solely to study and attended by students, exclusively male, from distant places as well as the town or city in which the yeshiva happened to be located. Moreover, these yeshivas were generally independently funded, and not controlled by the local rabbis. Transplanted to the New World, yeshivas have remained central to the persistence and growth of Orthodox Jewish communities after the period of mass emigration and genocide. Today, the largest Lithuanian-style yeshiva in the United States is in Lakewood, New Jersey, while many others are located in New York City, upstate New York, and elsewhere in the United States.

As understood by traditional Judaism, "Torah" encompasses not only the Hebrew Scriptures, but also a vast sea of rabbinic texts stretching back two millennia and still being created in the present, as well as authoritative verbal discourses pronounced by teachers today. As the epigraph from Deuteronomy suggests, the work of understanding Torah is understood as a profound mix of human freedom, discipline, and responsibility. If Torah broadly is understood as the word of God, the authority of those rabbinic texts and discourses derives from a combination of the labor, talents, and fear of Heaven their authors devoted to understanding that divine word and to activating it as a human inheritance. Thus, whether the subject of study deals with overtly "religious" matters or with rabbinic law governing business relations, the study itself is understood not merely as another intriguing "subject" like math or science, but as probably the single most central form of divine service to which a Jew can devote himself.

The core text studied in the yeshiva is the Babylonian Talmud, which includes the authoritative early compilation known as the Mishnah, and the record of subsequent centuries of debate and elaboration known as the Gemara. The rabbis whose dicta are recorded in the Mishnah are known as Tannaim, while those whose names appear in the Gemara are known as Amoraim. In the yeshiva, Talmud study is characterized by close attention to the text's commentaries, especially those of Rashi and Tosafos, dating from the later medieval period in northern Europe. Although they lived centuries after the talmudic text was more-or-less closed, their texts are printed in the margins of the Talmud itself, thus making them appear to the student as in some sense contemporaneous and in dialogue with each other. Typically, a fair amount of time is also devoted to leading compilations of Jewish law from the early modern period, especially the sixteenth-century *Shulchan aruch* of Rabbi Joseph Karo. Students may spend time studying biblical texts as well, although with some exceptions, Bible study is not an organized or central focus of the yeshiva.

This book describes my experiences studying at Mesivtha Tifereth Jerusalem, or MTJ, a yeshiva near my home on New York's Lower East Side. I do not mean to present MTJ as a "typical" or "representative" yeshiva. Partly because it is small and neighborhood based, and partly because of the distinctive heritage and character of the Lower East Side Jewish community in which it is located, it is more informally structured than most Orthodox yeshivas. During the years described in this book, in addition to regular Talmud lessons taught Monday through Thursday, there were also a weekday morning class in the modern compendium known as the *Mishnah berurah* and a weekly lecture in *mussar* (homiletics), but not all those who studied regularly at MTJ participated in these structured lessons.

I had spent a good deal of time at MTJ in the 1980s, but hardly stepped back in until late 2011. At the beginning of that earlier stint, Reb Moshe Feinstein, the father of our current Rosh Yeshiva, was still alive. Reb Moshe was the leading Orthodox Jewish *posek* (decisor) of his generation, famous at once for his rigorous devotion to Orthodox law, his flexibility in the face of changed circumstances, his personal humility, and his availability to the entire community. The unusual mix of traditionalism and unpretentiousness that still characterizes MTJ represents his legacy.

That much I have known for decades, and indeed, some explanation of the quarter-century gap between my earlier and current studies at MTJ may be in order here. In 1983, I returned with my spouse, Elissa Sampson, from a year of fieldwork among elderly Polish Jewish immigrants in Paris. Those Polish Jews were resolutely secularist, and Elissa and I were struck by the vast cultural gap between them and their children, who for the most part seemed well integrated into French culture and little attuned to the Yiddish language and east European Jewish culture of their parents. This helped shape our view that, in order to persist, Jewish identity in diaspora requires some sort of everyday frame to tell us what it is that Jews do and don't do. That, along with a long-standing desire to gain more literacy in the traditional rabbinic texts, led me to join an adult men's beginners' group at the yeshiva for a few years in the mid-1980s. Though I didn't initially conceive of my time there as fieldwork, it eventually led to some academic writing on the social character of reading.[1]

I stopped attending that group around the time my first child was born, and had hardly stepped into MTJ in the intervening years, when the wonderful good fortune of a full year's academic leave came my way in 2012—the year I refer to in this book as "my *kollel* year." In the interim, and with much delay, I had finally commenced a full-time academic career. When my year's leave began,

I was teaching at the University of North Carolina at Chapel Hill; a semester after it ended, at the close of the 2012–2013 academic year, I accepted a position at Cornell University in Ithaca, New York. Hence, I occasionally refer in this book to my various departures and returns between New York City and either Chapel Hill or Ithaca.

You will read, however, references to Chapel Hill coming sometimes after those to Ithaca. This is not a chronological narrative of how I found my place in the yeshiva. Through the generosity of new study partners, I found that place very quickly, even though it remains in some ways always provisional. Instead, the book is in some part a mosaic made up of vignettes or less, quick sayings, fragments of interaction, a form indirectly inspired by my hero Walter Benjamin's book *One-Way Street*. There are, to be sure, also discrete passages of analysis, but I have attempted to limit them so that they do not intrude overmuch on my portrait of the life of the yeshiva.

Commencing with an introduction that makes explicit some of the constraints shaping this project, addressed at once to the academy and to the yeshiva, I move on sequentially to descriptions of the scene where all this study happens; of the wider Jewish and general communities in which the yeshiva takes its place; of the patterns I and others follow in the daily rhythm of individual, shared, and group study; of the Rosh Yeshiva, or Rebbi, who stands as the moral and intellectual head of the entire yeshiva; of the various and tantalizing meanings of what study "for its own sake" might mean; and of my own image within the yeshiva. I conclude with a brief meditation on the relation between the rhythm of yeshiva study and the temporality of dreams.

My hope is that, if the yeshiva is an unknown place to you when you begin to read, it seems more familiar by the end; and if it is already a familiar place, you may be reading it in a new light and with enriched appreciation of its significance today. Remarkably, the yeshiva persists despite the severe decline in the Lower East Side's Jewish population and the loss of related infrastructure in recent decades. I hope this book will give you some sense of what it's like to study there. Along with many others who are identified only by pseudonyms herein, and who will, I trust, accept this as my collective expression of heartfelt thanks, I am especially grateful to Reb Dovid Feinstein, Rosh Yeshiva of Mesivtha Tifereth Jerusalem, both for his teaching and his gracious accommodation of the writing of this book.

YESHIVA DAYS

Introduction

A MOMENT OF shame nearly begins the notes I began taking some years ago for what was to become this book about study of rabbinic texts among other adult male Jews who are members of the *kollel* (full-time adult study corps) at MTJ. The moment was my first, and very brief, personal encounter with the Rosh Yeshiva—the man who for decades has been the moral, administrative, legal, and scholarly address of last resort at MTJ. Born in 1929 in the Soviet Union, he has been the head of this institution since his father's passing in the mid-1980s. He is himself regarded as one of the top Orthodox authorities on Jewish law in the world and continues to put in six very full days at the yeshiva, yet in many ways appears as a very private and almost shy person.

My presentation of self in the following brief encounter clearly reflects my nervousness about my place at MTJ, and perhaps some doubt on my part about whether I ever could really come to belong there. The vignette introduces Rabbi Simcha Goldman. Like many at MTJ, he is a regular there but also spends much of his time giving noncredit Talmud classes at various colleges and universities in the New York area. For that reason, I was referred to Rabbi Goldman when I first announced my intention to study at MTJ again. His mission seems to be introducing bright young men with less background to the beauties of Torah, and though I'm less young than most of his study partners, we still study together whenever our schedules permit. In this anecdote, Rabbi Goldman has given me instructions that I did not follow to my best advantage:

> *December 25, 2011*: Every Sunday morning at 10:15, the Rosh Yeshiva conducts a *shiur* [lesson] in *Mishnah berurah*, the commentary and compendium by the nineteenth-century rabbinic authority known as the Chofetz Chaim, covering the laws of everyday, Sabbath, and holiday practice. Unlike the Talmud shiur held in the library upstairs, this one meets in the cafeteria downstairs—perhaps because the crowd is a bit larger on Sundays. About fifteen men were waiting for the Rosh Yeshiva, and stood as he entered the cafeteria. I stopped him briefly as he approached the table to introduce myself, and then turned around and realized to my embarrassment that I had made everyone else stand longer than they would have had I just allowed the Rosh Yeshiva to proceed to his place. Rabbi Simcha Goldman, my first teacher at the yeshiva, had told me to introduce myself, but I suppose I could have picked a more opportune moment. Later, as I related this awkward moment to my son Jonah who is visiting from California, he said, "Well, of course you weren't thinking about that. How many situations are you in these days where people routinely stand up as a sign of respect when a certain individual enters the room?"

As it turned out, causing everyone in the class to remain standing while I introduced myself to the Rosh Yeshiva wasn't the only mistake I made in that encounter. Fortunately, I didn't become aware of the second cause for embarrassment until more than three years after the fact. In March 2015, I was in the middle of a dreary winter semester in Ithaca, dutifully pursuing my second read through of the entire Babylonian Talmud in the recent ArtScroll edition with English elucidation. Toward the end of tractate Sanhedrin (100a), I reached a passage that discusses what behavior makes one an *apikoros* (roughly, a heretic). Rabbi Nachman says it is one who calls his teacher by his name. I realized only then that when Rabbi Goldman had told me I should introduce myself

to the Rosh Yeshiva, he didn't say how. Not only had I made everyone else wait, but I had addressed the Rosh Yeshiva as "Rabbi——."
Even if I hadn't yet seen (or didn't remember) the talmudic warning telling me that wasn't the right way to address him, it felt
awkward. So why did I make these mistakes? Perhaps there was
something ritualistic about it—the faux pas that begins an ethnography, or (the same point put slightly differently) a semistaged
case of what I like to call "wrong ethnography," a scene in which
the ethnographer reveals some key aspect of the world being described by showing how he or she misunderstood it early on in the
encounter. Maybe in some way I set up my own miscue to drama-
tize that I was starting an encounter with something very different
from my usual routine, a kind of ethnographic *estrangement* that
may have seemed almost necessary in a situation where the passage from "home" to "field" is a walk of slightly less than a mile
down Essex Street.

Although I didn't introduce myself to the Rosh Yeshiva that
morning as an anthropologist, those who became my closest study
partners at MTJ certainly knew that was my profession. They
knew as well that I had written about the Jewish community of the
Lower East Side, and to the extent it mattered to them, were aware
that there was some chance I would be writing about them as well.
As for me, I remained unsure about my project, through the year
I studied more-or-less full-time at MTJ and beyond: Was I working as an anthropologist, or simply, in the discretionary time God
and the university had given me, fulfilling a traditional male Jew's
dream of engaging in intensive study? Was it possible to do both
at the same time?

Thinking of my time at MTJ as only for itself—a complex concept I will explore further in this book—certainly had its compen-
sations. It freed me to some extent from the anthropological
compulsion to note and comprehend everything happening
around me, clearly an impossible task given the multiple conversations going on at once in that big room, and even more so, the
infinite twists of the texts studied there. And even just one of my
study partners, Nasanel, shared with me day after day endlessly

convoluted verbal riffs that, were they jazz, would make me the greatest collector of the decade. As his study partner, I could admire these extended riffs while at the same time being frustrated at how little progress they allowed us through the very texts we were ostensibly studying—I, at least, for the first time. As an ethnographer, listening to them without recording them made me feel like a miner without a sieve, watching countless flecks of gold flow past my grasp toward the sea.

To be sure, Nasanel plays an outsize role in this book, much as his voice carries across the entire *beis medresh* (the "house of study," or study hall), sometimes to the annoyance of those who are just trying to quietly study a text. If I focus on him, it is not because he is a "typical" student at MTJ. Rather, it is because he has more directly challenged my secularism than other, more circumspect acquaintances have, because he is more interested in the specifics of my secular learning than some of them would be, and because part of what makes MTJ special is that it has room for his broad interests and startling juxtapositions. Of course, some of my other study partners are among those quieter students, and they are in this book as well; but there are many others who study diligently at MTJ and find themselves only in other books instead.

Nasanel was, in any case, also my prime confidant as I debated whether and how to think of making this book. On a Wednesday in October 2014—the afternoon of Hoshana Rabbah toward the end of the fall holiday cycle, after almost everyone had left the yeshiva and he was walking me back home in order to continue our conversation, I told him that I would probably write a book about the yeshiva. He said, "You should disguise it somehow—people are very sensitive. Say the yeshiva's on Henry Street," just one block further toward the East River than East Broadway. That, I pointed out, wouldn't help—there's only one yeshiva on the Lower East Side. Besides, its uniqueness and not its typicality is what draws me.

Later that fall, just back from Ithaca to begin my winter break, I mentioned to Nasanel that I was thinking further about writing a book about the yeshiva, and that I thought I needed to ask the Rosh Yeshiva's permission. This made him nervous, especially when I made clear to him that it would be an academic ethnography and not a book of fiction: "Hmmm . . . certainly your book would be mostly positive but there also has to be some negative to keep it honest, right? You know, in here he's pretty easygoing but he's a big figure in the Orthodox Jewish world, in the Aguda."[1]

I made clear that it wouldn't only be about the Rosh Yeshiva, but about the beis medresh as a whole.

"Well, then, you'd have to ask everybody's permission, no? And anyway, he might not mind, but the people in the office really won't want a book written about them. This isn't exactly a place that's looking for that kind of publicity."

I joked that I wanted Nasanel to ask for me, and he was relieved a bit later when he realized I wasn't actually asking him to. He still seemed to think it was risky. "Well, you're being extremely high-minded about this. Whatever he says to you, he'll be smiling. But what if he says no?" I replied that I'd be disappointed, but I wouldn't write the book.

This again made Nasanel nervous, not so much because I'd be risking Rebbi's wrath as because Nasanel wants to see my book. "And would you show him the manuscript beforehand?" I said I wasn't sure. I don't want to be censored, but by now it's not unusual for anthropologists to show their manuscripts to the people they're writing about before they publish. That surprised Nasanel in turn: "Wow, things must have changed in the past thirty years. Did you ever hear of a guy called the Central Park Guru? He's this guy who's been through literally every religion: now he's semi-Lubavitch. At one point they called him the Central Park Guru, and he had one follower who asked a lot of very blunt, in-your-face-type questions. It turned out that guy was a Columbia professor, and when he published his book, the Central Park Guru was really angry. When I first came here some people thought I was writing a book, because I asked Rebbi very blunt questions that nobody else would ask."

I told Nasanel I would be thinking about this some more, and that I would quite likely rehearse my explanation to Nasanel before going in to speak to the Rebbi.

I received a bit of encouragement from an unexpected quarter—the yeshiva's Mashgiach, a rabbi in his sixties, originally from California, who like most of those who work and study at MTJ, knows much about the wider world around him and remains uncompromising in his insistence on the primacy of our reliance on God. In the traditional Lithuanian-style yeshiva, the mashgiach's role is very roughly that of "dean of students": he supervises the course of study, makes sure students are being diligent, and tests them if and when they are ready to receive rabbinical ordination. He also attends to the shaping of their moral sensibilities. At MTJ, the last function is represented primarily by the Mashgiach's weekly delivery of a half-hour *mussar shmues* (moral discourse), a tradition that grows out of the nineteenth-century Mussar movement and that was once a more central part of many Lithuanian-style yeshivas. The *shmues* is generally closely tied to the weekly Torah portion, and that week the Mashgiach discussed the eternal question of why the biblical Joseph never sent word to his father that he was safe and prospering in Egypt. The answer: he was waiting to have his father and all eleven of his brothers (thus explaining the need to have Benjamin sent down from Canaan as well) bow to him to fulfill his earlier dream. Still, the Mashgiach asked rhetorically: Why was that so important? Joseph had interpreted Pharaoh's dream, and he then went on unbidden to proceed with advice for how to handle the coming famine and was duly appointed to carry out that advice. In order to demonstrate the validity of his dream-prophecies and thus carry out his famine mission, he had to see his own earlier dreams fulfilled as well. The moral the Mashgiach announced was that, if you see something, even something very ambitious or audacious, and it's a *davar tov*, a good thing—go ahead and do it and don't shrink, don't be too humble. As he was saying this, I was asking myself: Is the book I want to write about the yeshiva a *davar tov* or not? The answer wasn't clear in my mind.

Later, as I sat talking to Nasanel about how to approach the Rosh Yeshiva with my plan to write a book, he suggested, "Tell him not just what good it will do for you, but also that it will be good for the yeshiva, it will be good publicity." So evidently Nasanel imagined that it could be a *davar tov*. In the end, I wasn't able to get in to see the Rosh Yeshiva after shiur, but on the advice of his *gabbai* (secretary) Effi (who only knew I needed to speak to the Rosh Yeshiva, not about what) I approached the Rosh Yeshiva after minchah, the afternoon prayer service, and said, "I would like to speak to the Rebbi about a matter that concerns the relationship between my professional work and my study at the yeshiva." He replied that he wouldn't be in his office after shiur tomorrow, so he said, "Next week."

Although I had hardly exchanged a word with the Rosh Yeshiva since that day I had introduced myself, I had good reason to imagine he didn't consider me exactly the star of the class. My notes reflect my tendency to lose the thread of a difficult discussion and fall asleep during the shiur, if only momentarily. Some three months after I started going steadily, I wrote, "Today was I think the first time I didn't nod off at all in the Rosh Yeshiva's shiur. I sure didn't follow everything. Twice the older gentleman who sat next to me and had been chatting me up before the shiur nudged me and said quietly, 'How often does this kind of thing come up in real life?'"

A few days later, I again kept my eyes open through the seventy minutes or so of the shiur: "I didn't fall asleep at all in shiur today and followed much of the Tosafos—at least in the sense of knowing where the Rosh Yeshiva was reading. But I did find myself at one point in a near meditative trance, focusing on the patterns of white spaces between words on succeeding lines of Tosafos."

Occasionally, I felt I had a decent "excuse" for being less than perfectly alert, such as the day I attended the 11:00 a.m. shiur after driving from Ithaca and arriving in New York around midnight the night before.

More often than not, the times I lose the thread, the Rosh Yeshiva and a couple of the veteran members of the shiur are struggling over a subtle difficulty that I don't understand. Sometimes it seems as though I, and even some of the others who've been in the shiur far longer than I, are observers at a private study session mostly involving the Rosh Yeshiva and two of my regular study partners. Both are fathers of families, in early middle age. One, Yisroel Ruven, is a lifelong Lower East Side resident, deeply devoted both to the Rosh Yeshiva and to the neighborhood's Jewish heritage. He has piercing blue eyes, and, like several others at MTJ, a neatly trimmed beard. Like a true native East Sider, he has no hesitation in speaking his mind, whether the topic is neighborhood politics, the boundaries of Orthodox Jewish practice, or the plausibility of a given reading in a passage of the Talmud. The second, Asher Stoler, commutes to the Lower East Side every day from the eastern end of Brooklyn. More reserved, or at least less voluble than Yisroel Ruven, Asher almost never raises his voice except very occasionally in frustration when a study partner fails to reach what he believes to be proper understanding of the Gemara. He takes detailed notes at the Rosh Yeshiva's shiur, kept in the margins of his own volumes of the Gemara and in notebooks left by the windowsill, though I wish he would at least make photocopies of them for safekeeping.

As my mind wanders while they debate the fine points back and forth, I sometimes have brief daydreams that are vivid and tangentially but suggestively tied to the actual conversation—such as an image of a group of learned and observant Ashkenazic Jews in the mountains of North Carolina in, say, the early nineteenth century.

There doesn't seem to be any particular stigma about catnapping at some point in the midst of what can be a ten-hour day devoted to study, as there certainly was, for example, in the law office where I worked for several years when I was younger. One morning I arrive around ten fifteen. Asher was learning with the somewhat troubled high schooler he'd been supervising. Our fourth regular study partner, Hillel, was there as well. Hillel, then a young man in his early twenties, not yet married and at that time unsure about his own career goals, was dozing over a *khumesh*, the Five Books of the Torah with Rashi's commentary. When he woke up I said, "That's impressive—it's hard to sleep that long with your chin resting on your arm like that."

He replied, "You have to be really tired."

By the spring of 2015, still attending shiur whenever I was in New York, I made some progress in both attention and comprehension. One day I noted: "Progress: Even when I don't understand what they're talking about, it's still not as meaningless to me. Or maybe that's just because I got up later and didn't go to the gym, so it's easier to stay focused this morning." And yet, even then, there were days, especially after a long absence, when returning to the beis medresh was painful because I felt both so far behind and so inconsistent in my attendance. On such days, retaining the sense of belonging suddenly required a great effort.

Noting particular preferences and concerns of my fellows in the beis medresh is probably one of the easier ways to retain that sense of belonging—certainly more feasible than suddenly becoming an expert interpreter of the more abstruse commentaries, or performing the kind of ideological makeover that would make me more of a *kollel* insider and less of an anthropologist. One morning I walked into the beis medresh and presented Yisroel Ruven with the gift of some very expensive and very fancy dark chocolate from Guatemala that's marked "OU pareve," to indicate its kashrut supervision and status as neither dairy nor meat. He had mentioned—as I understood—a year or more previously that he liked dark chocolate and would love to have some fancy chocolate except that he only eats *cholov yisroel*, dairy products that are not only kosher but handled and produced by Jews.[2] It was a good investment: he not only made clear at the time that he appreciated it very much, but later on (after shiur), when Hillel and I were learning on our own in Asher's temporary absence, Yisroel Ruven came over and spent some time with us clarifying key points covered in the shiur. I don't mean to suggest that he wouldn't have helped us but for the chocolate. But still.

Perhaps keeping good notes, during the times that I do so, is also a way of belonging. My study partner has a notebook; so do I. But I kept my yeshiva journal only sporadically, and there are no notes for several months of the year I attended full time. Why I kept notes for some periods and not others, I don't know very well. I don't even understand very well why there are periods when I am conscious of the value of note-taking but there seems nothing to report. Sometimes, as during the semester I was teaching a seminar on Jewish ethnography at Cornell, the texts I assigned to my class helped by reminding me of the importance of the mundane rather than the extraordinary in ethnography. Other times it was indeed hard to know what to note other than, "We spent several hours studying a very difficult text." What is the anthropologist to do when it's impossible to take field notes on discourse in the field—not because the cultural performance is so ineffable, subtle, or sensual, but because the cultural "text" depends on a literal text that is barely accessible to the ethnographer?

Then too, even though its sensibilities and its history are deeply embedded in the specificities of the Jewish Lower East Side, the camaraderie of study at MTJ is focused almost exclusively on the time everyone spends together in the room. Unlike some yeshivas, the beis medresh at MTJ is not the focus of an all-encompassing community.[3] Thus, my tentative thoughts of furthering some of my yeshiva friendships outside its walls hardly took shape—with the significant exception of the many times Nasanel walked me home to the East Village before returning to the yeshiva by himself.

At the beginning of one summer I had mentioned to Yisroel Ruven that I would be going back and forth to Ithaca, and would like to stop off and visit him at the bungalow colony in the mountains where his family spends the summer. He countered with a suggestion that he'd like to see Ithaca. Elissa and I were in Ithaca in fact for two weeks in July, but I never contacted him to invite him, and I kept thinking afterwards about my failure to do so. It seemed like it would require too much organization, such as buying a new grill and having him bring the meat for a barbecue so as to meet his standards of kashrut. Even more so, I didn't want to address the fact that my observance of kashrut at home would likely not be sufficient for Yisroel Ruven's family. But I was also thinking: What will I show him? What will we talk about? Is there enough for us outside the yeshiva?

Since those who come to study at the beis medresh are offered informal assistance with finding study partners, but not "placed" within any rigorous system, it is common enough to see someone studying by himself, and perhaps like me, he may not always be happy doing so. One year on the Fast of Esther just before Purim I found myself unaccountably lonely, wanting very much to sit with Asher and Hillel as they studied the laws of Purim, but for some reason too shy to ask.

Of course, Yisroel Ruven and I could study together anywhere, not just at the yeshiva. Indeed, one recent summer when he was away in the country with his family, he kept up his studies by telephone with Asher, while the latter sat in his usual place in the yeshiva. But perhaps when this book is published, it will be another bridge for conversation for us outside of the talmudic text. I have already had some indications that the book is eagerly awaited by at least some at MTJ. At the annual kollel dinner in May 2015, months after I had gotten the Rosh Yeshiva's permission to do so, I told Asher about my project. He seemed delighted. I told him he could have any name he wanted, and after musing a bit, he somewhat shyly asked me if he could be called by his actual name. Though that request seemed reasonable, I did tell the Rosh Yeshiva I would change names. And Yisroel Ruven had warned me early on: "If you write a book, just don't use my real name."

So there are risks, of the kind alluded to by Holmes and Marcus in the epigraph to this chapter when they refer to "the politics of knowledge that any project of fieldwork involves." Surely a key aspect of those politics consists of rules for inclusion and exclusion: who may choose to join the subject community and who may not. One implicit requirement for anyone who wants to study at MTJ is that such person be identified as Jewish. More troubling, from the perspective of a discourse committed to the expansion of rights and opportunities to all without regard to gender, is that study at MTJ is only available to males. That exclusion surely must be noted, but otherwise I will not attempt to address it here, let alone reconcile its self-evident justification in the eyes of my colleagues and teachers at MTJ with its likely repugnance to several of my academic colleagues, and perhaps some other readers as well. Moreover, since study at MTJ is an exclusively male realm, and I am not attempting here any study of the home life of its denizens, the women who surely make it possible for their husbands and sons to spend so much time in unremunerative study remain largely invisible in this book.

I do not think it is especially helpful, in any case, to think of this is as a book written *about* the members of a religious "world" for the members of a secular world. Certainly, the university—in my case, the University of North Carolina at Chapel Hill, where I worked during the first year I spent at the yeshiva, and then Cornell University, where I work now—and the yeshiva have their own distinct and demanding codes. Both, like the very different institutions on which Holmes and Marcus focused their attention, are institutions whose reason for existence is the production and transmission of expert knowledge. And while MTJ focuses on exoteric rather than "secret" knowledge—on a Torah that is in principle to be shared with all male Jews, at the very least—it is also an institution that relies on the loyalty and discretion of its regulars. Accordingly, there are profound limits to my service as a source of secret knowledge for the academic anthropological community—on general ethical grounds, to be sure, but more pressingly because I want to continue to belong at the yeshiva. Similar considerations in other ethnographic contexts have produced the notion of what the Native American anthropologist Audra Simpson calls "ethnographic refusal,"[4] which for my purposes may be described here as the right and sometimes the responsibility of both ethnographers and those about whom they write not to tell everything that might be of interest to the academy as presently constituted. The right of ethnographic refusal is one of the conditions of possibility of what we call auto-ethnography, which in many cases, and not just this one, is properly a form of undoing. As the Gemara itself warns:

> There was this student regarding whom a rumor emerged that he revealed a matter that had been spoken in the study hall twenty-two years earlier. Rav Ami expelled him from the study hall and said: "This one reveals secrets." (B. Sanhedrin 31a)

1

The Big Room

NEARLY ALL OF the activity described in this book takes place in two rooms, one carved out of the other. The beis medresh boasts several great arched windows facing directly onto the sidewalks of East Broadway. It is furnished with bookshelves across the back, except where doors open onto the vestibule, and on the front right side as well. The remainder of the front wall, to the east as Manhattan geography is understood, is taken up by a large Torah ark, and then, approaching the East Broadway wall, by three desks. The desk closest to the ark, shielded in sagging plexiglass, is left untouched as a relic of the former head of the yeshiva. The middle one is the desk of the current Rosh Yeshiva, though for many years he has spent most of his time, when not teaching or praying in public, in a small office across the foyer. The desk closest to the windows belongs to the Mashgiach. In the middle of this big room stands a *bimah*, the platform from which the Torah is read on appropriate occasions. Those who animate the room with their study sit at several rows of metal tables, laid out along the axis between East Broadway and the interior courtyard, with seats facing in both directions to facilitate face-to-face study in pairs or slightly larger groups. They are all male, consistent with standards of modest comportment that dictate general segregation of males and females in public, and with the traditional Orthodox view that women are not obligated in Torah study generally, nor is it seemly for them to study Talmud. While a woman might briefly enter the beis medresh on a matter of urgent business, it is unusual for her to do so. When the beis medresh is used for Sabbath and holiday prayer, however, the side of the room away from the street is separated off by a curtain and becomes the women's section.

The smaller room is called the library, though there are plenty of books on the walls of the beis medresh itself. Here the Rosh Yeshiva holds his 11:00 a.m. and 2:00 p.m. Talmud classes. One day, while we sat waiting for him to enter the room, I said, "This is a good room [the library]."

Yisroel Ruven responded, "Yeah, there's been a lot of Torah learned here. Before it was the library, it was the [previous] Rosh Yeshiva's office. And originally, it wasn't a separate room at all—the beis medresh was just one big symmetrical room."

When the library is not being used for a formal class, individuals or pairs of students will sometimes come in to have a quieter place for themselves, or to conduct personal business by phone. The books on the library shelves are organized by categories, such as "Commentaries on the *Shulchan aruch*." As with most libraries, some books are consulted frequently, others much more rarely.

The books that receive the heaviest use, the volumes of the Babylonian Talmud, are shelved on the rear right side of the beis medresh, right behind the table where I most frequently sit with my study partners. While there are a few nearly complete sets, most of the Talmud volumes are individual tractates gathered over the years. That they come from a wide range of printings generally matters little, since the standard layout of these tractates was established in Vilna in the nineteenth century, and generally continues to be observed by printers today. When I started coming regularly in late 2011, there were piles of books on top of these high bookcases, and a few volumes I had brought from home were added to those piles. The Rosh Yeshiva's son-in-law Rabbi Karp, who manages the everyday running of the beis medresh, often sat at the other end of our table, either by himself or with a study partner who might sometimes be me. Looking at the volumes on top of the bookcases, he reminisced: "People used to come in and complain that they're covering over the [memorial] plaques" for deceased ancestors that supporters of the yeshiva have donated over the decades. And when I recorded that reminiscence, I thought to myself: "If they don't do that anymore, it's probably because the relatives who paid for the memorial plaques aren't around anymore themselves."

More recently, new bookshelves were installed, along with new overhead lights, flooring, and chairs. The new lighting was especially welcome given the countless hours members of the yeshiva spend poring over fine print. A rather grandiose chandelier in the center of the room seems less functional and more of a nod to the recherché notions of respectability that characterize Orthodox Jewish neighborhoods such as Borough Park, Brooklyn. For several months after the renovation, the tops of the bookshelves were clear, and all of the memorial plaques were legible, if anyone took a moment to read them. By late 2016, the books were inevitably piling up again, since there was no place else other than the tabletops where one's own books might be stored. Indeed, there is precious little in the way of "personal space" in the beis medresh at MTJ beyond, perhaps, one's accustomed but not necessarily guaranteed usual seat.

For the most part, everyone is tolerant of this lack of space, but an occasional expression of annoyance may be heard. One time, Hillel tossed an article of clothing from the windowsill across the table, and complained about people who just leave their stuff lying around. I asked what it was. It turned out to be my own cap, which I'd left there a week earlier.

Some regulars at the yeshiva may be present, seated at the same place, and indeed studying the same text, from 10 a.m. until after 6 p.m. every weekday except Friday. Others may come and go more frequently or may study in different parts of the room with different partners over the course of the day. Various pairings and small groupings assemble for study regularly, occasionally, or just once. When I began my kollel year, every morning before the Rosh Yeshiva's shiur, Asher was with Yisroel Ruven, Hillel and me in the back by the window; after the shiur, he might be back in the same place with Yisroel Ruven, or around 1:00 p.m. as part of a group with a brilliant young ex-NYU student named Isaac Maxon and others. Who, I wondered, moves and who stays in the same place? Who joins and leaves whom? Who seems to wander around the beis medresh holding random if erudite conversations in English much of the day?

The tables in the shelter of the bookshelves where Yisroel Ruven, Asher, Hillel, and I sat that year are, as it were, one "neighborhood" of the beis medresh. One morning, shortly after I sat down with Hillel and Asher, there was a noisy interchange coming from the tables on the side of the room toward the front and furthest from the windows on East Broadway—that is, the corner of the beis medresh diagonal to and furthest away from where we sit. Though I recognized the voice of the loudest speaker, I couldn't tell what the discussion was about. I knew it wasn't necessarily an argument, since yeshiva exchanges can be vociferous without hostility. Another time I distinctly heard one of the Rosh Yeshiva's adult grandsons ask on the other side of the room: It says, "'You shouldn't sleep more than a horse sleeps.' How much does a horse sleep?"[1] I realized that if I had been sitting on the other side of the beis medresh, these notes would constitute a very different ethnography, one might say, an ethnography of a very different place.

Toward the front of the beis medresh, in a table close to the Mashgiach's desk, a Cornell history alumnus in his thirties named Max Greenberg and his *chevrusa* (study partner) were sitting together and studying for the oral exams given by the Mashgiach to see whether they were ready for *smicha* (rabbinical ordination). Then came the exams. I watched from the back as they sat and conferred with the Mashgiach for a couple of hours. As they finished and the Mashgiach was walking past me, I asked Nasanel: "Does he tell them right away how they did?" and then noticed that the Mashgiach was right there and had probably heard me ask this nosy question. . . . Oh well.

Later, several of us went downstairs to the cafeteria, to share the same food that had just been served to the schoolchildren at MTJ's "lower" yeshiva next door. At lunch, I asked Max how it went, and he said, "This part—not so good. But he won't tell us if we passed until it's over." Talk at lunch was nevertheless about Max's impending smicha, and how long he'd been at it—seven years, which everyone joked about being a very long time. Max mentioned that the fastest time he heard of someone successfully studying for smicha is eight months. One year is considered fast. Perhaps to soften the suggestion that Max had taken too long preparing for his exams, someone pointed out that the weekly Torah portion was about Pharaoh's dream of the seven years of plenty in Egypt (only it's also about the seven lean years as well, of course). The same person was talking about organizing a big party to celebrate Max's smicha, but Max didn't want to take the outcome for granted yet.

In fact, Max did pass. I tried to get him to tell me whether there would be some kind of smicha ceremony, or if he would just get a piece of paper. He planned to stay at the yeshiva, at least for the time being. "Well, I might get some part-time work," and indeed, shortly after, he began teaching in the lower school at MTJ.

Meanwhile, out in the big room, my space is in the front corner because that's where Asher Stoler and Yisroel Ruven sit, and because when I first arrived, at Rabbi Goldman's prompting they had invited me to prepare the daily Talmud text with them. This gives me a vantage point on some moments of the yeshiva's routine where one or both of them is a key player. One of these is the annual procedure in which observant Jews, in preparation for Passover, formally transfer all of their *chomets* (leavened goods) to a non-Jew, who then inevitably transfers it back after the holiday ends. This accomplishes the requirement that chomets "not be seen and not be found" in the possession of Jews during the holiday. Rather than each household arranging the transfer directly, one member of the community, commonly a rabbi, will be designated as their agent.

Thus, before Passover in 2014, I noted:

Once again, Rabbi Stoler is handling the sale of chomets for anybody who wants to take advantage of his services (and sometimes receives a tip for doing so). I asked him who he sells it to, and he said, "Ramon," the custodian. It's a long ceremony; he takes it very seriously—he wears a suit. He does it two times on one day [for those going to Israel for the holiday, who need to have their leavened items sold before they depart] and two times the next [before the holiday itself begins]. And we go through every form of *kinyan*, every form of legal sale according to Jewish law. One year he said, "No, I'm not signing that— we're not done yet!"

Rabbi Gavriel Pinsker, a resident of Passaic, New Jersey, who comes for the Rosh Yeshiva's shiur each morning and then heads to his job teaching computing for accountants at Baruch College, added a story of his own about Ramon: one time after minchah (the afternoon prayers) there were a number of men who had come from the Orthodox community of Lakewood, New Jersey, waiting to ask the Rosh Yeshiva *shayles*, questions about religious law. Ramon asked one of them what his shayle was. So, the guy looked at him funny, but then asked him. Ramon thought for a second, looked at him and said, "You better ask the Rosh Yeshiva that one."

Between the entrance doors and the bimah there's one table. Here the Rosh Yeshiva conducts his morning class on the Mishnah, but otherwise, it's sort of a neutral zone where anyone has equal rights. Anyone who has snacks for the group—often slightly stale pastries, leftover bagels, or the roasted peanuts I would bring when I returned from Ithaca, until they were banned as an allergy risk—will most likely leave them on the back table. That table itself is a subtle marker of shifting levels of stricture in the Orthodox community. Officially, our yeshiva still follows Reb Moshe Feinstein's ruling that dairy products require only an ordinary kashrut certification, and not the designation of *cholov yisroel*, which indicates dairy products handled only by Jews. Thus, one morning

FIGURE 1.

I noticed an empty package of Little Debbie brownies, a mass-produced and prepackaged brand, on the table next to us. Hillel told me that about a month earlier, some people from Brooklyn had been in on Shabbes, and had marveled at the package of Oreos (which carry a certification from the Orthodox Union, but are not cholev yisroel) on the windowsill, as though it were something exotically old-fashioned. On the other hand, one time when I brought in a package of peanut-butter stuffed pretzels with an OU but not cholov yisroel designation, Rabbi Goldman removed them from the back table, and left them out in a less conspicuous spot with a note in large letters warning, "Not cholov yisroel." This was an indication that, by now, enough of the regulars or occasional visitors to MTJ might be observing the greater level of stringency so that leaving "ordinary" dairy products out would be inconsiderate.

One morning there was a pile of chocolate-filled donuts on the back table in honor of Chanukah. I knew I didn't need the carbs and don't particularly like chocolate filling (I prefer the Bavarian cream), but gave in to the temptation and took a half eventually. They were stale. I remarked to Asher and Hillel that it's amazing—only at MTJ could we get stale donuts on the first day of Chanukah.

Hillel said, "Yeah, before you came in I mentioned to Asher that they don't look very fresh."

Asher added, "Don't be shocked, but I think they might have been frozen from last year."

The back table is also where occasional "drop-ins" are most likely to sit. One afternoon Nasanel spent a couple of hours at the back table in animated philosophic conversation with an elderly gentleman in worn but clean street clothes, who didn't seem *yeshivish* at all but was clearly a fluent reader of the Hebrew Scriptures. One of them announced: "I learned philosophy in Athens, in the school of Socrates. Where did you learn it?"

The old man referred to a phrase he heard in a dream— something like "Gibr-milta," though I don't remember it well now, which he interpreted as a combination of words in Arabic and Aramaic. Nasanel insisted this was a dream that demons brought to him; if it were a true dream, the words would have been in Hebrew. Still insisting on the value of dreams, the old man said: "There was a man in the Land of Israel who had a dream during the 1920s that all of Europe was in flames. Then he went around trying to warn everybody, but nobody would listen to him."

Nasanel: "My great-grandfather read the newspaper in the '20s, and saw Europe in flames, and he got his family out."

The old man read out of a book of Psalms to give a lesson in physics. "And this is very relevant to understanding *Star Trek*. The past, present, and future are all coexistent, they're all there. That's why the Psalm [19:3] says *yom le-yom yabiye omer*—one day speaks to the next [so they must be coexistent]. On the other hand, the only way we can get to the future is in a straight line."

———

Go back out the doors, and you'll find yourself in a modest foyer with a high ceiling, arched in neo-Moorish style, though decorated with nothing except more plaques, this time naming donors rather than the deceased. From the entranceway to the building, a set of stairs leads up to the elementary school and the high school, though these are gated except when the students are headed down to the basement cafeteria for their lunch. I have never been in those upstairs classrooms, and the only time I've seen them was the time Nasanel convinced me to climb the fire escape all the way to the roof and we peeked into the classrooms through the windows.

Even though I didn't see the doors leading into those classrooms, I do know that on each of their doorposts there is now a kosher mezuzah, the tiny box containing brief, handwritten scriptural passages that fulfills the biblical requirement to "write them on the doorposts of your house." A kosher mezuzah is one that has been properly calligraphed on prescribed parchment, and whose letters are all intact and legible. I know that the classroom door mezuzahs at MTJ are kosher because of a story Mike Harris told me one day. Mike is a middle-aged, devoutly Orthodox man who runs a modest computer consulting business, dresses in a way that only reveals his religious affiliation because his head is always covered, and lives in the Village View houses near us, on the northern edge of the Lower East Side. Mike's sons, about seven and ten years old at the time, attended the lower school at MTJ. He told me that the previous year there had been an odd coincidental series of accidents in which boys had gotten hurt. Some of the parents eventually suggested that the mezuzahs should be checked (on the notion, popular in the Orthodox community, that bad things happen to children when mezuzahs aren't kosher). The Rosh Yeshiva was asked permission to check the mezuzahs, and he responded: "No. The halacha is that they don't need to be checked, and we don't have the money to fix them." So the parents raised money to have the mezuzahs fixed if necessary, they were checked, and indeed several of them weren't kosher. I can't be entirely sure, of course, why Mike chose to tell me this story, but I'm guessing it was for the same reason I found it memorable. That is, part of what makes the Rosh Yeshiva a remarkable figure is his adherence to the Lithuanian tradition of rational Judaism, as against some of the mystical or "magical" trends that have gained increasing popularity in some Orthodox communities in recent decades.

To find the administrative offices, you have to leave the beis medresh, go out the foyer onto East Broadway, and then reenter the building through the next set of doors—assuming you aren't willing to bother the Rosh Yeshiva, whose office opens onto both of these buildings. One day, I mentioned to Nasanel that I really wanted one of the old-fashioned MTJ *pushkes* (charity boxes). These green metal boxes are about five inches high, three wide, and one deep; they have a coin slot and a lock at the bottom that can only be opened at the yeshiva. The photographs on the front and back appear to be from around 1960, one showing a diligent, large class of boys around ten years old, with corduroy pants and plaid checked shirts, and the other a group of younger boys at mealtime, wearing either brimless caps or large yarmulkes sectioned in alternating white and colored patterns, like fraternity beanies. These pushkes bear a legend in Yiddish urging the reader to contribute coins to support the yeshiva. I suppose what I find especially appealing about them is the combination of Yiddish text with a photograph of children who, with the exception of their head covering, look entirely like other New York City children in those years.

Nasanel said he had seen a whole box of them in the yeshiva office recently. I got him to go there with me. To get there, we had to go out onto the street and in through another entrance, where we found two women inside the beis medresh hard at work, along with Rabbi Nobel, the yeshiva's financial administrator. Malkie the secretary told Nasanel there weren't any of the old pushkes available, and so Nasanel pushed through to Rabbi Nobel, where he got the same response. "But I saw a whole box of them here!"

Rabbi Nobel replied, "Rabbi Schoenstein, go back to learning!" Nasanel remonstrated some more, until Rabbi Nobel said, "Nasanel, you know I love you, or I would have kicked you out years ago." Sending Nasanel back to the beis medresh brought home how the notion that separating out the place where administrative (and especially financial) functions are carried out from the place of adult study (the beis medresh) reinforces the impression that study at MTJ is done purely for its own sake, about which I'll say more later in this book.

The nature of the beis medresh changes not only according to where one is seated, but over the course of the day. I typically arrive shortly after 10:00 a.m., by which time my study partners have already begun to prepare for the shiur to begin at 11:00 a.m. At that time, after the morning prayers, which I attend elsewhere, there is often only a sprinkling of men sitting and studying. Over the course of the morning, the numbers increase, cresting at several dozen in attendance for the minchah afternoon service. Then many hurry out, perhaps to their jobs as teachers in the lower school, and a few even back to work on Wall Street. Several of the most diligent, truly full-time kollel members continue to sit and study until around 6:00 p.m.

In early 2012, a few weeks into my kollel year, I wrote to a close friend:

Depending on the day (but it's basically Monday through Thursday), I'm studying a bit of Gittin [the tractate that deals with divorce law] for an hour first with a couple of guys in their thirties or so, married and very friendly, and I have no idea how they can afford it; then I go to the shiur on that same part of Gittin that's given by the Rosh Yeshiva; then I study [the classic late medieval/early modern legal codes] *Tur/Shulchan aruch* for an hour and a quarter with yet another guy who's on winter break from a gig giving shiurim to college students; and there's another rabbi who might or might not have time for me on a given day, depending on how long I'm willing to stay. I think the only time in the week everybody in the room is supposed to be doing the same thing is for *davening* [group prayers] and then for the weekly *mussar shmues* on Wednesdays before minchah.

The mussar shmues I referred to above and in the introduction, delivered by the mashgiach, indicates the yeshiva's heritage within the Lithuanian Jewish tradition of combing intensive Torah study with discipline in morality and scrupulous self-examination. While the mussar component is not as heavily emphasized at MTJ, or, I believe, elsewhere in the yeshiva world, as it was in its heyday in the nineteenth century, concern for character development is still reflected in certain areas such as scrupulous respect for the personal property of others.

One Wednesday around 12:40 p.m. the Mashgiach entered the beis medresh, approached his desk, and set a heavy *sefer* (religious book) down with a bang. Everybody looked up, a bit startled, since a hand slapping the table announces the beginning of the mussar shmues—but that doesn't start until 1:00 p.m. This turned out to be a false alarm.

At 1:00 p.m. precisely, the Rosh Yeshiva, sitting at his desk in the front of the beis medresh next to the Mashgiach's desk, announced a *siyum*, a public completion of study of the massive tractate Bava Basra. Minimal in its ceremony, this consisted of nothing but the very last few lines of the tractate recited and translated. It was followed immediately by the Mashgiach's mussar shmues, this week dedicated to the memory of the Rosh Yeshiva's father, whose *yortsayt* (death anniversary) was that day. The Rosh Yeshiva listened from his desk at the front of the room.

The Mashgiach related a talmudic analysis by Reb Moshe Feinstein, concerning the technicalities of a guarantor of a loan and the need to avoid his being deemed to have earned interest, which is forbidden by Jewish law on a loan to a fellow Jew. Why should there be any concern that a guarantor receives interest? What benefit does a mere guarantor have? On the contrary, he's at risk. The answer: a guarantor, says Reb Moshe, is someone who is a *ne'eman*, trusted by the court the way Moses was trusted by God. And this trust of the court, which regards the guarantor as a *ne'eman*, provides the guarantor with a considerable (moral or psychological) benefit. A guarantor, a *ne'eman*, is someone who will go beyond the letter of the law to take care of fellow Jews.

The Mashgiach added two stories about Reb Moshe's faithfulness, his *ne'emanos*, told as reminiscences of his childhood friend Reb Boruch Epstein. At the bungalow colony where the Epstein family and the Feinsteins stayed in the summer, Boruch's father finished studying *khumesh*, the Five Books, with his young son, and made a siyum. He didn't invite Reb Moshe because he felt this was too small a thing to trouble the latter. The Rosh Yeshiva showed up anyway: "Why didn't you invite me, after all it's a siyum!" Later that summer, when the family left, Reb Moshe ran after the car to see them out. That, concluded the Mashgiach, is a *ne'eman*—someone who does what God wants even where our books don't tell us what to do.

On another occasion the Mashgiach gave two mussar shmuesn in one week, because that week included the fast of the Tenth of Tevet, the date on which the siege of Jerusalem leading to the destruction of the First Temple is said to have begun. His language is a rich and familiar blend of Yiddish, English, and the Hebrew-Aramaic mix known as *loshen koydesh*. On this fast day, his ultimate point was that the surest way to gain merit for the World to Come is to be *mezake es harabim*, to do good work on behalf of the community. The journey to that point involved a wealth of citations from older mussar literature, including one by an author he referred to as Reb Itsele Peterburger. This turned out to be Reb Yitskhok Blazer, one of the inspirations for the Mussar movement, who did indeed live in St. Petersburg, at a time when the right to live there was granted to very few Jews. Along the way the Mashgiach considered the problem that it's hard to know whether you "use up" the merit of your good deeds in this world, leaving little for the World to Come.

Another anecdote from that day's shmues stuck in my memory. The Mashgiach recalled a visit some years ago to the widow of a prominent Orthodox rabbi from Los Angeles. She was already about ninety years old, and limited in her capacities. He asked her how she was doing, and she said, "I want to die."

"So I protested—I told her, 'What do you mean you want to die? You can still pray and recite Psalms, you have your whole family who still want you around and value you. . . . But she said, 'gelebt heyst gelebt far yenem—dos iz nisht keyn lebn.' Life means living for others—this is not a life."

It's not clear how other listeners "read" or are affected by these stories and these moral lessons. No one has ever suggested to me that, for example, they had now decided that the truest form of Jewish devotion was directly helping others, rather than the study of Torah. Implicitly, it seems, the assumption is that those who have the privilege and discipline of full-time study are *mezake es harabim*, benefiting the community, by contributing to the overall store of merit derived from Torah study that the Jewish collective can claim on its own behalf in "negotiating" with God for its own welfare. Otherwise, mussar shmuesn like this one seem to stand as a reminder of the deeply active and transformative concern with personal morality that marked an earlier phase in the history of the institution known as yeshiva, as a source of stories about moral exemplars in the past.

One day Nasanel and I wanted to keep studying the Mishnah together even after the mussar shmues began. Rabbi Karp, who suffers in the heat, had already moved to the library to study because the air's too close in the beis medresh. Nasanel and I found chairs and sat in the hallway. Nasanel, noticing that the mussar shmues had begun, discreetly reached his hand in to close the door between the beis medresh and the hallway. Sure enough, ten minutes later Issachar Dov, a volatile regular who takes care of various practical matters pertaining to the beis medresh, made a point of not only opening the door, but scolding us for making too much noise.

As we were heading out after the shmues, Issachar Dov was having a loud argument with Yisroel Ruven. Effi, the Rosh Yeshiva's attendant, passed by the shouting Issachar Dov, and called out in a moderate voice (not sotto voce, but also not loud enough to make sure Issachar Dov would hear), "Jesus loves you."

Shortly after 1:30 p.m.—thus, on Wednesdays, after the mussar shmues ends—everyone gets up from his books, while others file in from the lower school and from the street to recite minchah together. We begin when the Rosh Yeshiva joins us. By then I'm at my prayer station right next to the bimah, where one would think the Rosh Yeshiva has to pass by to get to the front. Yet somehow I usually don't notice him coming in: he's not there and then he is.

There's a crowd of between about fifty and seventy men in the beis medresh for minchah, a strong majority in suits and black hats, though by no means all. I do not dress like them for my time in the yeshiva, though in the course of a few years I've taken to the minimal discipline of putting on a white, button-down cotton shirt every time I go. During the service, a few of the younger men, including Asher, circulate with collection boxes for various causes within the Orthodox community.

The Amidah prayer, or "Eighteen Benedictions," is shortened at MTJ during minchah. Rather than giving everyone the time to recite the prayer to himself, followed by a repetition out loud by the leader that includes the section of sanctification known as Kedusha, the leader recites the first phrases aloud, and continues through the Kedusha, following which everyone recites the entire prayer to himself. When I reported this to the rabbi at Cornell, he found it curious, so one day I asked Rabbi Karp the reason for this practice. Rabbi Karp told me that the previous Rosh Yeshiva held it as a *minhag*, an accepted tradition carried over from Reb Chaim, founder of the great yeshiva in the small town of Volozhin, halfway between Minsk and Vilnius in today's Belarus. There are two justifications for this somewhat unusual practice: first, it saves time for study (the Talmud says that scholars engaged in study only have to recite the biblical minimum of prayer); and second, it may be assumed that in the yeshiva everyone knows how to *daven* (recite the prayers) for himself, and thus does not need to listen to the full repetition by the leader. Moreover, Rabbi Karp explained that the minchah prayer is recited early at MTJ, in order not to have minchah and lunch be two separate interruptions of learning, even though in principle, a later minchah might be preferable because it is closer to the time of the late-afternoon sacrifice in the Temple in Jerusalem, the ritual for which afternoon prayer is said to substitute.

There are usually a few men reciting the Kaddish memorial prayer at the end of minchah, and Rabbi Karp is always one of them. I found out why one day, when my friend Sam Lemberger, owner of the Second Avenue Kosher Deli, called while Elissa and I were on our way back from visiting cemeteries in Long Island. His bookkeeper's mother had died, and he wanted me to arrange for someone to say Kaddish for her throughout the coming period of mourning. The next day in yeshiva, I asked Asher if this was a task he'd take on. He told me he couldn't, because his parents are still alive, something I should have realized myself. He told me to ask Rabbi Karp, who agreed to do it in exchange for a five-hundred-dollar donation to the beis medresh.

Another distinctive practice at MTJ, although again not unique, is the pronunciation of the last vowel in the words "Who makes the wind to blow and the rain to fall," inserted into the Amidah during the winter months. The grammatical dispute turns on whether this is the end of a sentence or not, and that in turn determines whether one pronounces the word for rain as "geshem" or "goshem." Yisroel Ruven expressed views about this one day:

> Some years ago, some guy found an old siddur [prayer book] that had "geshem," and he claimed it was grammatically right, and he went around collecting signatures from rabbis that we

all should be saying "geshem." He got to Reb Moshe after he'd gotten a lot of signatures. Reb Moshe wrote a *teshuva* [a legal responsum] that he may be right, but that the pronunciation of "goshem" is also defensible, and since we've been saying "goshem" for so long, there's no good basis for changing it now. So that's the minhag of the yeshiva, to say "goshem." One time the Rosh Yeshiva's grandson was davening for the *amud* [leading the service], and he said "geshem." I called out "goshem," but he didn't really hear or understand. I'm going to change it [in the prayer books that are used by people who lead prayers at MTJ]. When I was in Israel, there was a crazy guy who used to daven at the Wall, and he'd shout over and over, "Geshem! Goshem!"

The anecdote illustrates something about the way scholarship, critical inquiry, and the weight of authority interact at a place like MTJ. It is possible, that is, for a rabbinic authority to agree that, if one were faced with a question for which there was no existing answer in practice, the answer might go one way. On the other hand, where there is a practice in place and it is not clearly and unambiguously wrong, the weight of minhag might tip the scales against making a break and switching to the technically more correct practice. Yisroel Ruven's closing line about the "crazy guy" in Israel suggests as well that sometimes it may be better not to obsess overmuch about these relatively detailed matters of pronunciation or other questions of form.

Every day there's a lunch break right after minchah; a sign on the door to the basement cafeteria says: "Beis Hamedresh lunch 1:45 to 2:30 sharp." About fifteen or twenty of the adults and young men go down to lunch, and one day I joined them for the first time. The very simple lunch that day was the same as the schoolboys have: chicken noodle soup that tasted like it was heavily boosted with artificial broth; sandwiches flavored with very thin slices of meat and roasted peppers; sliced cucumbers and yellow peppers; baked beans; applesauce.

There I found a Jamaican cook, whose name, as I learned, is Ulysses, come to assist the Hasid who's been the cook for years. As he handed up the trays of food he called out repeatedly, "Good stuff! Good stuff!" Saying this, he echoed Ramon the Dominican custodian, who in turn first heard this call of "Good stuff" from Rabbi Feld, a yeshiva regular who's a hasidic resident of Williamsburg, Brooklyn, and often arranges some food on days when the cafeteria is closed, especially during the summer. One year on Thanksgiving, since the yeshiva kids only have half a day, there wasn't much for lunch. Ulysses put out tuna fish and rolls, saying "Light stuff! Light stuff!"

Though more recently I'm likely to leave right after lunch, during my kollel year I often stayed well into the afternoon. One day I observed Rabbi Feld passionately repeating, over and over and fairly loudly, a slow hasidic melody, and sometimes actually whistling a chorus of the same melody—though I had always heard that Jews consider whistling to be a Gentile custom. As my wife Elissa's grandmother, Elizabeth, herself the youngest daughter of immigrants from Galicia, said in one of the few Yiddish phrases she recalled for us, "A goy fayft, nisht keyn yid" (A gentile whistles, not a Jew). Or, as the great Yiddish folk poet Mordechai Gebirtig put it in his song "Reyzele," "dos past nor far zey" (that's only appropriate for "them"). Apparently that supposed distinction between "them" and "us" has been relaxed among the hasidic communities in America.

Another afternoon I studied with Nasanel until around 4:45 p.m. Though I was a bit tired, I had a dinner date in Chinatown at 6:00 p.m., so I decided I might as well stay in the yeshiva for the extra hour. I asked Asher if he wanted to review the Gemara a bit more, and he said, "Soon." He was working through something just then. So, I sat at the table and continued my solitary study of the section of the *Tur* that deals with marriage and family law, with Asher at one end of the table and Max Greenberg, looking at the *daf yomi*[2] in the ArtScroll Gemara, across from me. About 5:15 p.m. Max said, "Rabbi Karp doesn't have time for you?"

I replied, "No, Rabbi Stoler doesn't have time for me." I didn't mean to chide Asher but I couldn't resist.

Asher turned to me and said, "I was just trying to finish up this Tosafos here, but why don't we learn together for a bit now?" And we reviewed the passage we'd studied in shiur that morning once again, seeing some things in a new way that makes more sense.

Just as the day has its varying rhythm, so too does the week. My most consistent days of attendance are Monday through Thursday, when the Rosh Yeshiva holds his Gemara shiur. But I was present one Friday, and then the following Sunday, when I noticed several fathers studying with their young sons. At least for this brief period toward the end of the busy week, these men were fulfilling the commandment to teach their children directly, rather than just seeing to it that others in the community were able to carry out that task. One day, the pair were a heavyset father whom I've seen before but don't know personally, and a son perhaps six or seven years old. I heard the phrase *bor bereshus harabim*—a pit in the public domain, which is from the tractate Bava Kama, one of the first pieces of Gemara young students study. It makes sense that Fridays (when some fathers might not be working, but in any case the boys get out of school early) and Sundays would be the day to see this. These moments where both men with full-time work "outside" and younger boys all find their place inside the big beis medresh indicate the kind of affective ties that would make families loyal to MTJ and to the neighborhood for generations, even without the overarching communal structures that, for example, hasidic groups across the river in Williamsburg sustain.

My notes trace in part the rhythm of the academic year at the yeshiva as well. While there are no formal terms, at least the Rosh Yeshiva's morning Talmud shiur corresponds roughly to the academic year of any secular university, beginning at the end of the summer, ending at the beginning of the next, although with breaks following the Jewish ritual calendar and virtually none to mark the end of the secular year.

A year and a half after my kollel year, at the end of my first year teaching at Cornell, I made a point of coming back from Ithaca to New York for Labor Day weekend. I might have done so anyway, but what was uppermost in my mind was being able to catch a couple of days of the Rosh Yeshiva's shiur. Someone had told me a couple of weeks earlier that the shiur would begin on the first day of the Hebrew month of Elul (as is the tradition in many or most yeshivas). But I might have remembered myself that at MTJ, the shiur actually starts the Wednesday after Labor Day. Perhaps I can be forgiven for not remembering, since when I came in and mentioned this to Hillel, he said that the Mashgiach had noted the distinctive pattern at MTJ as well, since he had begun one of his mussar shmuesn by saying, "Rosh Chodesh Elul, when the *zman* starts—or here, actually, after Labor Day."

There were very few people in the beis medresh that day—convenient enough because half of it was unusable just then. New lighting was being installed over the summer, and workmen were also plastering and painting the ceiling and walls.

On a Sunday some time later, I went down to Chinatown to get my broken eyeglass frames replaced by an optician who's long been active in the Lower East Side Jewish community. He was reading a magazine as he waited for customers, and he mentioned to me, "There's an article here about the last working wooden telephone booth, I don't remember where it is." Then he added, "There used to be telephone booths in the hallway at MTJ too, until they took them out. The phones didn't work, but Issachar kept all his stuff in them, so they didn't want to take them out." (There are finally coat racks there now.) Then he went on to tell me about all of the renovations he had supervised:

The flooring—it's not carpet, it's a rubber mat that looks like carpet. It's really tough, and all you have to do is wipe it down with something wet to clean it. The chairs don't make any holes in it. The new windows, I did that. The central heating and air conditioning, too. And the new lights. They're OLED, organic

LED. They used to run east-west, now they run north-south, to match the tables. They cast two-thirds of their light down, one-third up, so the white ceiling shows really nicely. I tested the lumens when they were deciding where to put them in, so there wouldn't be any checkerboards (patterns of lighter and darker areas). There's one more fixture that has to go in, right over the bimah. I wanted it to be a bent OLED, so it would be like the Clouds of Glory [that followed the Jews as they wandered through the desert]—but they want to put a big chandelier in there instead, like the Hungarians. Alright, so they'll put in a chandelier.

I got that report some time after the work was finished. In late summer 2013, the work was still in progress. A few days after my pre-Labor Day disappointment that the shiur had not yet started, those present included Mendl Feld, a retired kashrut supervisor from Brooklyn named Rabbi Weiss, and just a few others. Mendl Feld tapped his fingers and repeated in a sort of hip-hop rhythm:

Vi zenen di yungelayt?
Vi zenen di yungelayt? (Where are the young married
    students?)

The occasion for his question became clearer a few minutes later, when he started singing in Yiddish about how nice Elul *zman* is, when the *bokhurim* (unmarried students) come back. Of course, this was actually a bit sarcastic, since it was already the fifth of Elul and the bokhurim weren't back yet.

Later he was singing some Yiddish words I couldn't make out to the tune of "Oyfn pripetshik," a sentimental chestnut that recalls the warmth of the traditional *kheyder*, the Hebrew school of eastern Europe. "Oyfn pripetshik / brent a fayerl" (In the oven a fire is burning). A few minutes later, Rabbi Weiss was humming the same tune to himself, and then across the room another older regular picked it up as well. Later I come closer, and Mendl wanted to make sure I caught the words. Rabbi Simcha Goldman had arrived, and Rabbi Feld was singing

Oy ven Simcha kimt
Brent a fayer do. (Oh when Simcha comes, a fire burns here.)

I had first learned Rabbi Feld's name when I began studying with Rabbi Goldman, though I think I've known him since the 1980s. He came over to say hello, and turned to me: "So how'd you get to learn with him [Simcha]? I've been waiting for years to learn with him."

I answered, "That's your problem. You've been waiting here, and I went away for twenty-five years, so now that I came back I get to learn with him." Simcha introduced us, and I said, "Yeah, we haven't talked much, but we know each other a long time already."

On Labor Day itself, the very day after Mendl Feld wondered aloud where the young people were, the yungelayt had returned, or at least it felt more like the usual crowd when yeshiva is in session. As I came in around 10:30 a.m., Asher was telling Hillel stories about a *sheva brokhes* (part of the weeklong cycle of postwedding celebrations) his mother-in-law had recently attended. "My mother-in-law is sitting behind this big *mechitzah*," a partition separating men and women, "and there's this guy she can't even see telling these awful mother-in-law jokes, and she can't believe it. If it was me, I'd think, maybe for this crowd that joke's not right, but he just gets up and says it. And they keep asking him back!" An example: "There's a knock on the door, so the guy opens it. 'Shviger [mother-in-law], what a nice surprise! How long are you planning to stay?' 'As long as you want me to.' 'You mean you won't even stay for a cup of coffee?'" Here, Asher was once again functioning as a native ethnographer, remarking on the limits of acceptable discourse in a public situation, and carefully taking his distance from what he saw as a conventional but actually unacceptable denigration of the women of his community.

Another time, Asher took the opportunity to underscore how he values MTJ for holding on to reasonable standards in areas such as kashrut, rather than giving in to the trend of ever-increasing stringency that seems to characterize much of the Orthodox world. I had brought in a box of cookies a friend had brought us from Gideon's Bakery uptown (bearing the impeccable kashrut seal of the German Jewish Breuer community) and put them on the front table. Mendl took them to the corner where he and Reb Volf sit, with the justification, "They'll last longer here." They went very fast nevertheless. I brought them back over to our table a bit later, and urged Asher to take one, as a reward for figuring out a difficult comment by Rashi.

Zach from Brooklyn (a regular attendee at the Rosh Yeshiva's shiur, who'd come in that day because he thought shiur was going to start), wondered aloud what blessing should be recited over a kind of very thin cookie that doesn't really seem to be made of dough and that Asher had taken. Asher said, "Ask Rabbi Karp [who is indeed the person you'd ask at MTJ about the proper blessing to recite over various kinds of food]. He'll say, 'No brokhe [blessing] is necessary.'" Then Asher explained, "I'm just joking. [But it's true that] Rabbi Karp tries very hard not to put chumras on people, not to force them to adopt stringencies."

Somehow this spirit—of resisting the general trend toward increasing stringency within the Orthodox world—is linked to both a deadpan, streetwise humor and to a greater willingness to exhibit awareness of "outside" cultural references than one might find elsewhere in the yeshiva world. Since so much of what draws me at MTJ is tied to that spirit, I note as many moments of its appearance as I can, and I list a few more of them here:

> At lunchtime one day, someone pointed out that we had latkes for lunch on Chanukah and also today, December 25, subtly taking note of the fact that December 25 "also" is a major holiday, and thus gently tweaking the efforts religious groups take to maintain rigid boundaries between themselves.

Another day Levi Kurtz, who sits and chats with Asher sometimes after lunch, was looking at a kosher supermarket circular. "Chicken loaf," he read aloud.

I asked, "What's chicken loaf?"

He answered, "You sort of take pieces of chicken and smush them together into a loaf. . . . I don't think you're supposed to eat it." Perhaps, on reflection, what Levi meant was that there was some kind of problem with the kashrut of chicken loaf; but I took it as an entirely deadpan suggestion that this particular item was actually inedible.

Yet another day, in another part of the room, I passed by Mendl Feld, sitting with his regular chevrusa, Reb Volf, the son of the Rosh Yeshiva. Mendl had lately made a point of greeting me in friendly but perhaps slightly teasing Yiddish, and now he demanded: "Why didn't you say hello to Reb Volf?"

I answered (truthfully as it happens, although I rarely converse with Volf), "I did say hello to him. I reminded him about the deaf people who used to go around in the subway."

Mendl: "When was this—before the *krig* [war]?"

Me: "Depends what war you're talking about."

Mendl: "Every day I have a war with my wife. . . . Yeah, I remember them too, if you didn't give them money they took the cards back."

Another fellow standing nearby, who had been following the conversation, picked up on the "wartime" bit, reminiscing about a *Dennis the Menace* TV episode in which a neighbor keeps reminiscing about fighting with Lee. Dennis wonders how this man could be old enough to have fought with Lee, until the guy refers to "my wife, Lee."

Nothing would be remarkable about this anecdote were it not for the fact that television is increasingly banned from traditionalist Orthodox households, so much so that very few full-time yeshiva scholars would freely admit to having watched *Dennis the Menace* as a child. Similarly, another day, as I got up to go, something prompted me to quote to Asher and Hillel the old line associated with the character Wimpy in the *Popeye* cartoons, "I would gladly pay you Tuesday for a hamburger today."

Asher related that one day Itzy Hecht, a middle-aged rabbi in the neighborhood who often comes in to spend some time studying, turned to him and said, "I would gladly pay you fifty cents on Tuesday for fifty cents today" (presumably for soda, since MTJ has the last fifty-cent soda machine in Lower Manhattan).

At this, a very yeshivish [long beard, dark suit] type of guy who was visiting the beis medresh and sitting nearby said, "Very good" [i.e., very clever, indicating that he recognized the source]. Then the yeshivish guy confided that once he had been at an affair with his wife, and he quoted an old line from TV like that one from *Popeye*. At that, his wife told him not to refer to such lines—people shouldn't know that he used to watch TV. Still, none of the regulars seem embarrassed by what they know, including the comic books we read when we were kids. One day Yisroel Ruven turned to Asher and said, "Asher, let me puff up your yarmulke a bit—you look like Jughead!"

All of these are bits, and they must remain so, for there is no underlying "pattern" or "structure." If anything, the ethos of the place consists in relentlessly taking things as they are, and perhaps in some shared notion of a common sense that once prevailed among Jews and may have been connected to less attachment to outward signs of particularist belonging than prevails in the Orthodox community now.

Occasionally, without soliciting the information, I would receive bits of insight into how MTJ might fit into the constellation of nonhasidic yeshivas in New York and Israel, nearly all of which are larger and more institutionalized than is MTJ today. One day Asher told us that he'd been telling his son for years that he wants him to go study at the Slobodke Yeshiva (in Bnei Brak, Israel, a stronghold of the most strictly traditionalist yeshivish communities). "All the great ones came out of Slobodke—Rabbi [Yaakov] Kamenetsky, Rabbi [Yitzkhok] Hutner. And my son is like, 'Dad, what's this thing about Slobodke?' So now, he's starting his first year at Torah Vodaath [a well-established yeshiva in Brooklyn], and they put him together with a chevrusa. And one day he said to the guy, 'What do you think about learning at Mir [a yeshiva with branches in New York and Israel] next year?' And the guy said, 'My father wants me to learn in Slobodke!'" In fact, Slobodke is only one of several yeshivas in Israel where strictly Orthodox young men from America might wish to spend time; others include the yeshivas of Mir, Brisk, and Ponevezh, all named for the cities in eastern Europe where they were originally located.

Later, a reference to the commentary titled *Hagahos utsiyunim* led to the humorous reading of the second word as *tsiyoynim* (Zionists) and to Hillel telling about himself: "I was at [the] Mir [Yeshiva]. So one day I walked in with a knitted yarmulke with an Israeli flag on it, and I started getting these looks. Somebody says to me, 'that's a *tsiyoyni* yarmulke,' and I'm like, 'yeah, I'm a tsiyoyni,' and I didn't understand why they were all getting so mad at me."

This led to Asher's commentary: "Yeah, I used to think there were all these groups—there were [the black hats], and they were holy, and there were the Hasidim, and there were the Modern Orthodox, and there were even these guys with long hair and the multicolored clothes [Hillel: 'Yeah, the Braslaver' Hasidim], and they were all holy [and people understood that]. But now—it's like MTJ's the only place [where all of these groups can be tolerated together]." And he concluded in a mock-dramatic tone: **"We're the only ones left—it's just us three here at MTJ, man."**[3]

Thus, at least within the beis medresh, there's a sense of MTJ as a uniquely tolerant place within the range of Orthodoxy, which is sometimes accompanied by a willingness to deflate some of the currently conventional marks of excessive piety. One day while I sat by myself struggling to stay afloat in the sixteenth-century halachic work *Yam shel Shlomo* (Solomon's sea), I overheard Rabbi Pinsker reviewing the material just covered in the Rosh Yeshiva's shiur with another gentleman, an Israeli from a non-Ashkenazic background, who regularly attended the shiur. Rabbi Pinsker was explaining a difficult Tosafos we'd just reviewed, concerning the case of someone who gives his wife a bill of divorce while her hand is closed in a fist.

Pinsker: "He jams it into her closed hand."

Other gentleman: "What's 'jams'? Like jelly?"

Pinsker: "No, he jams it in—he *shtups* it into her hand."

Me, from nearby, interjecting: "He stuffs it in."[4]

Other gentleman: "He stuffs it in! Good! Simple English. [To Pinsker] If you don't know Yiddish, don't talk Yiddish."

Here was a non-Yiddish speaker, acknowledging the prestige that fluency in Yiddish has in the Ashkenazic yeshiva world, but gently suggesting that Yiddish shouldn't be used primarily as a mark of insider status.

A sense of no-nonsense, then, along with a sense of intellectual freedom, albeit a freedom whose bounds are quite different than they are in the secular academy. Indeed, the claim that there is intellectual freedom at the yeshiva might seem naïve to those who do not know the yeshiva world, and to many who have fled it as well. Some, such as Nasanel, acknowledge why it might not suit some people's tastes. Pursuing one of his favorite themes as he tries to make me more faithful to Torah, he repeatedly tries to convince me of the validity of divinely commanded mass slaughter or genocide in the Bible. Nevertheless, he told me of an elderly friend of his, a World War II resistance fighter who's nearly a hundred years old. This older man is religious, but had never studied the book of Chronicles. In studying Chronicles with Nasanel, they came to the story of Saul's slaughter of the priestly city of Nov for giving David bread: "A Hitler! It's not for me," and the older man walked out of the beis medresh. To be sure, Nasanel is somewhat unusual in his ability or willingness to "see both sides." One might describe this as characteristic of the place, or as particular to Nasanel; but it might be most accurate to say that MTJ is the kind of place where someone like Nasanel can fit in, and I can, too.

Some may come to MTJ because it is the only yeshiva left on the Lower East Side, and others may come from greater distances because they appreciate flexibility in exactly what, when, and how they study. Yet, from a certain perspective, what's special about the place is that it opts for continuity rather than marketing. The result is a sense of authenticity, much as that term is rightly scrutinized by cultural critics. At the kollel dinner one year, an honoree named Rabbi Avrohom Biderman who works at ArtScroll told a story about an off-the-beaten-path Hasid from Borough Park who had asked him about yeshivas that might be appropriate places for him to sit and study in kollel. Rabbi Biderman suggested he check out MTJ. He did, and though he decided that the commute wasn't possible for him, he told Rabbi Biderman, "Those [people at MTJ] are real Jews!"

Or perhaps, rather than that fuzzy word "authenticity," the better covering idea is simply, "We have been around for a long time." One day in the Rosh Yeshiva's shiur, we were discussing a passage in Bava Kama (70b) trying to decide which of two disputants, "Father Chalafta" and Rabbi Yochanan ben Nuri, held which of two opinions reported by Chalafta's son Rabbi Yose. Someone ventured the suggestion that either Rabbi Yose or his father was the disciple of Rabbi Akiva. The Rosh Yeshiva said, "They could both have been *talmidim* [students] of Rabbi Akiva, father and son. Certainly I've had talmidim father and son. Maybe even grandfather, father, and son. Listen, I've been teaching for sixty years."

While no one who attends the Rosh Yeshiva's shiur is younger than eighteen—and the beis medresh is designed, ideally, for those continuing on in advanced rabbinic studies beyond high school age—sometimes the younger boys from the elementary or high school are present in the beis medresh as well. One year there was special attention being given to a boy of about twelve who was having some trouble in school. Adults in the yeshiva took turns learning with him during the day, in a rotation for which Asher took responsibility. Yisroel Ruven commented, "Yeah, we'll try a different approach with him. Love and respect. He'll show us all up. We'll be going to his shiur some day." I can't tell whether this was said sarcastically, or with genuine recognition of the frantic intelligence and energy that seemed to be driving this boy's misbehavior. There's no reason, I suppose, why it couldn't have been both.

One day Asher showed me a chart he'd made up for this kid, so that he could get check marks for various behavior and study points. I told him, "If you don't watch out, people are going to hear you're good at this and you'll turn into a problem-kid learning rebbi."

Asher replied in mock panic: "Please, don't tell anybody! That's the last thing I need."

Another day two boys who had been suspended, around eight or nine years old, were hanging around the beis medresh, loosely supervised and advised by Hillel. It wasn't clear to me why they came to school, but it increased the sense of the beis medresh as serving, among other things, as a refuge or resource for kids from the lower school who need something additional or aren't fitting in to the regular classes. Still, their presence was a distraction, and eventually even Asher shooed them away.

A few months later, two other boys burst into the beis medresh and came up to Hillel, arguing bitterly, the larger one leaning heavily on the smaller one. The big one claimed, "I borrowed five dollars from him, and I paid him back. And now he took five dollars out of my pocket." The smaller one claimed he had no memory of being paid back.

Hillel tried quoting a relevant Gemara to them, but the younger one said, "I don't understand what you're saying."

Then Hillel said, "Go ask one of the rabbis."

Instead Rabbi Weiss proposed, "I'll give him [the bigger boy] $2.50, then you [the smaller kid] give him $2.50, okay?" That seemed to satisfy both the claimant and the defendant. Without detailed resort to any relevant rabbinic law, and without a judgment on the facts of the case, the smaller boy agreed to give back half of what he had taken, while the bigger boy wound up with (at least!) five dollars. Sure, it cost Rabbi Weiss $2.50, but that presumably was less money to him than it was to the boys. And we got to go back to our studies.

The Neighborhood, the City, and Beyond

A Child in Russia

As indicated in the previous chapter's references to still-thriving yeshivas named for modest towns such as Mir and Slobodke, the modern Ashkenazic institution of the yeshiva was created in eastern Europe. By now, of course, nearly everyone at MTJ was born in the United States. However, the Rosh Yeshiva (may he live and be well) was born in the town of Luban, in Belarus, and came to New York with his parents as a child in 1936. Very occasionally a reference in the Gemara or a question by one of the participants in his shiurim will elicit a brief memory of that distant time and place. Thus, tractate Gittin (at folio 73) includes a dispute among the rabbis over whether contracting parties may insist on fulfillment of the terms of a deal even when unforeseeable circumstances (here, a river becoming blocked) make it impracticable; the common-law concept of force majeure applies in analogous situations. The sage Rava, rebuking colleagues who were insistent that the terms of the contract remained enforceable in such a case, somewhat enigmatically calls them "white geese." This brought to my mind the extraordinary aggressiveness of geese, as reflected in the sarcastic Yiddish response to an idle threat: "strashe di genz"—meaning go threaten the geese. (I'm not scared, and they won't be impressed either.) I remembered, from a journey through Provence decades ago, watching a goose maliciously harass an utterly harmless old horse who had been put out to pasture. The Rosh Yeshiva, likewise, seemed to interpret Rava's "white geese" as an observation that his colleagues were trying to fleece their partner in the deal: "Actually the geese are a good example [i.e., analogy]. The geese in the streets of Luban used to come and pick at people."

Another time the Rosh Yeshiva indulged in a few minutes of jokes at the end of the shiur, drawing on the end of a long and complicated comment by Tosafos to Bava Kama 14b. The text discusses the case where "a cow damaged a garment [*tallit*] or a garment damaged a cow." Tosafos note that an alternate version of the text reading, "a cow damaged a sheep [*taleh*] or a sheep damaged a cow" must be incorrect. The Rosh Yeshiva mused: "Can you imagine what a monster that sheep would have to be [to cause damage to a cow]?" He commented further that, unlike his childhood in Luban, children today don't usually see animals like horses, cows, and sheep. "The only time you see a horse on the Lower East Side is Rosh Hashanah," referring to police security when the Jews of the Lower East Side gather en masse (although a smaller masse each year) at the East River for the ceremony of tashlich, where Jews symbolically cast their sins into the water. Thus, if there are fewer occasions on which Jewish children see farm animals or work animals, there are also fewer Jewish children (at least on the Lower East Side) who see the animals even then.

How to Get to the Yeshiva

From my apartment building, on the corner of Avenue A and East Third Street, turn right to head downtown. Cross Houston Street, below which Avenue A continues as Essex. Continue on Essex past Canal, cross East Broadway, then turn right for less than half a block to 145 East Broadway.

I count 1,500 paces from the corner of Canal and Essex to my door at 141 E. Third Street. MapQuest says it's 0.78 miles from my door to the yeshiva.

Very occasionally the yeshiva will come to me, such as one Friday, just a few weeks into my year in kollel. Although the Rosh Yeshiva gives a popular one-hour shiur on the weekly Torah portion, I didn't make it down. Nor would I have expected any of the guys who come from out of the neighborhood, especially on a short winter Friday. Anyway, I had to sit in my car for an hour or so to assure my parking spot on this day when New York's alternate side of the street parking rules were in effect.

A lifelong Lower East Side resident named Gershon Morgenthal, who makes part of his living as a dealer in rabbinic texts, called me at about ten thirty, just as I was getting ready to get out of my car. "I've got nearly all of the volumes for you. When can I drop them off?" I had pledged to complete the set of the ArtScroll Babylonian Talmud at my synagogue on Stanton Street, and Gershon was able to get religious books at a good price, as long as you were willing to wait a while until he actually gets them. "So when do you have to go back [to North Carolina]?" he asked me when he arrived at my building.

I explained that I was in New York for the whole year, on research leave.

"So what are you researching?"

"Gittin," I replied as a joke, since that's what the Rosh Yeshiva is teaching. But he took me seriously:

"Ah, so that's why you're regularly at the yeshiva now. Well, good, *mitokh shelo leshma ba leshma*, from doing it not for its own sake you'll come to do it for its own sake." I explained that what I really meant was that I have a lot of free time on this research leave, so I decided to spend much of it at the yeshiva.

"Ah, so you'll be writing something out of it. Not, I mean, that you wouldn't be doing it anyway." There was no censure in his tone, and in fact, he went on to remind me of William Helmreich's book, *The World of the Yeshiva.* "You haven't read it? You really have to! He did a nice job; it wasn't nasty. Of course, that was quite some time ago. Remember, we've only really had yeshivas here for sixty-five years [thus, Gershon was dating the beginning of American yeshivas from the end of World War II]. In the fifties and sixties we had to try to drag guys out of public school to go to yeshiva. Now . . ." Gershon didn't have to finish that sentence. Clearly, he was referring to the greatly increased number of Orthodox Jewish children sent to boys' yeshivas and to Orthodox schools for girls, a development spurred both by the internal dynamism of the community and by the perceived decline in the quality and safety of the public schools.

That dynamism is not very much in evidence on the Lower East Side, however, for reasons that have been debated for decades and seem to have much to do with larger real estate patterns and especially housing pressure in Manhattan. Fortunately, as mentioned, the beis medresh at MTJ draws men from outside the neighborhood as well. Once a young man whom I didn't recognize came in and greeted various people whom he clearly hadn't seen for some time. He explained that he'd taken the day off from work because he hadn't been in the yeshiva since the summer and needed a dose of the place. Downstairs in the lunchroom, he kibitzed about how happy he is in Brooklyn and how much he hates to drive in Manhattan:

> Those taxis are always reaming you. I was going to B&H [Photo, a prominent hasidic-run business], and I wound up in a lane on Thirty-Second Street where I realized I was heading for the tunnel. I figure, no way I'm going to New Jersey! I had to back up. But there are all these cars behind me, and they refuse to back up. So this big *goy* [Gentile] gets out of his car and says, "Back up a little bit!" I was saved by a goy. I used up some of my *zchus* [accumulated merit in the divine reckoning]. But I hate to use it up on things like that.[1]

"How to get to the yeshiva," of course, can also be a question about the contingent itineraries that lead various individuals to become so connected to an institution outside their home neighborhood and community, and whose advantages are not immediately obvious.

Here's what Nasanel said to me about how he wound up at MTJ. We were talking about Graham Greene's novel *The Third Man*. I mentioned the movie, and Nasanel said he had seen it. This led to a reminiscence about his "youth" (he's not exactly old now), when he had studied at the "right-wing" Kamenetz Yeshiva—a term that, in this context, may refer to increasing strictures about the separation of men and women, enforcement of modest and distinctively Jewish dress codes, extrastringent standards of kashrut, or carefully policed avoidance of aspects of secular culture. In this case, Nasanel mentioned that at Kamenetz students could be thrown out for things like watching movies. He was living in Riverdale, where his father had a rabbinical post. The yeshiva in Riverdale was run by the German Jewish community known as Breuer, after one of its leading rabbis. Someone who had powerful connections at Breuer made sure that Nasanel wouldn't get accepted there, because he was opposed to Nasanel's father's appointment as rabbi of his Riverdale congregation. As a result, Nasanel was sent from the Bronx to Borough Park, Brooklyn, for yeshiva—a very long commute by subway.

> Otherwise I would have become a regular YU [Yeshiva University] intellectual. At Kamenetz, I realized where mainstream Orthodoxy was going, and with all of their stringencies they were turning people into liars—things were forbidden, people did them, so they lied. And I tried the Israel thing, I went there a couple of times, but I realized that what's happening there isn't the preparation for the coming of the Messianic era. I also tried various hasidic groups: I tried Bobov, I tried other ones—I figured just because one was bad it didn't mean the others were bad. Plus, I didn't want to learn another language [Yiddish] in order to be in a yeshiva. People go to Israel, they understand a few words and they fake the rest. That's not how you learn. You

have to be precise, and it's very hard to do that in a new language. So I told my father I was looking for a place where they study Gemara seriously, and eventually he suggested I try our Rosh Yeshiva. So I came to a shiur, and now I've been here seven years.

Unlike some larger yeshivas, especially perhaps those in Israel, there do not seem to be any formal recruiting efforts at MTJ. Only once, when I remarked how capable and pleasant a new member of the kollel seemed to be, did the person I was speaking to reply proudly, "Yes, and I got him to come here." Other than those who are from the neighborhood, I would venture that people find their way to MTJ either because of the Rosh Yeshiva's reputation as a leading authority on Orthodox Jewish law, or because, like Nasanel, they have somehow gotten the sense that the place will be right for them.

In any case, not everyone who comes ends up staying that long. During my kollel year, one of the regulars was a fellow whom I named, in my book about the Stanton Street Shul, Isaac Maxon. He had fairly recently joined the yeshiva world after nearly completing a BA in computer science at NYU, and his fluency and diligence both astonished me. When my brother Daniel, a professor of Talmud at Berkeley, came to the yeshiva with me one day, I reintroduced him to Isaac, who had come to visit when we sat shiva for our mother. Isaac said, "He's almost a member of the kollel here." (In fact, Yisroel Ruven had said of me, months earlier when he was urging me to come to the kollel dinner, "and you're a member of the kollel.")

> Daniel: "Yeah, give him the same salary and he'll quit North Carolina and stay here permanently."
> Isaac: "The benefits are much better here!"

Isaac moved to Queens shortly afterward, and he was much missed. So I was delighted to see him in the yeshiva around the time of the fall holidays in 2014. Perhaps, I thought, he was just visiting his in-laws for the holiday—or perhaps he had returned. He came up to say hello, and I said, "You light up the place."

Asher added: "Yeah, actually the lights are just the same as they always were" (that is, and it's not a change in the light fixtures but Isaac's presence that makes the place seem so much brighter).

I saw Isaac again a couple of weeks later, and then again when I stopped in during the Thanksgiving break. Finally, I asked Hillel whether Isaac was back full time. Hillel explained to me that Isaac was here mornings to learn with a father and son (separately) who were congregants at Hillel's father's shul, and who were paying Isaac to learn with them. Hillel said that Isaac might in any case be moving back into the neighborhood since his wife (a member of a prominent Lower East Side rabbinical family) wanted to live here again, but as far as I know, they never did move back to the Lower East Side.

Perhaps a year after I noticed Isaac Maxon back in the beis medresh, I returned from a semester at Cornell to see three young hasidic men from Williamsburg sitting and studying together in Yiddish at the end of our table. Hillel told me that they were here studying for smicha (rabbinic ordination) from the Mashgiach. They were studying the laws pertaining to slaughter and the kashrut of animals. They were two brothers and one brother-in-law. Hillel thought it was interesting that they were here, since they looked like "mainstream" Brooklyn Hasidim. "But I realized once they were here for a couple of days that if they weren't scared off by the place's unconventionality, they would probably stick around. After all, it takes a few years to get smicha, so by the time they've been here two years they'll really be part of this place." Later I was told that the Mashgiach was unhappy with the idea that there was no one studying for smicha at MTJ, so he found these three Braslaver Hasidim[2] and convinced them to sit and learn there. As of the end of the summer of 2017, they were still regulars.

The Neighborhood

The people who came to the Lower East Side and the people who were born here created a network of institutions that has been gradually dwindling for decades, while the yeshiva stands out as one of the survivors.

Yisroel Ruven is in the "born here" category. As I realized quickly, I had actually met his father, Eliezer, just a few weeks before I started going regularly to the yeshiva. Eliezer is a volunteer with Lower East Side Hatzoloh, the local branch of the independent free ambulance and EMS service. Eliezer had been in our home unexpectedly over Thanksgiving weekend, when a Sabbath guest suffered an attack of sciatica so vicious she was unable to move from our couch. I was very impressed by his "gentle but firm" manner on that occasion, since he was able to convince her to rise from the couch despite the pain it caused her. So, when I saw him at minchah in the beis medresh, I greeted him warmly, and then he smiled broadly, pointed to Yisroel Ruven, and said, "That's my son." And Yisroel Ruven pointed back to him and said, "That's my father." I couldn't be sure, of course, that just because the father lives on the East Side the son does too, but I learned that was in fact the case.

By contrast, Asher Stoler lives out at the far end of Brooklyn. One day he arrived late, and clearly exhausted; his wife was away in Israel that week. "When they go away, you find out how much they do. It's incredible. You think they don't have that much to do, but there's so much."

Another regular at the beis medresh, tall, middle-aged, thin, reserved, and very pious in manner, hearing about my mother's death, asked me her Hebrew name so that he might have permission to study halacha in her memory. Hearing more about how I came to the yeshiva, he put his hand on my shoulder and blessed me, "May you become the biggest *talmid chacham* [rabbinical scholar] that Hashem wants you to be." I quickly learned that his name was Rabbi Cantor. Rabbi Goldman had mentioned a couple of times that the seat next to his is "Rabbi Cantor's," but I hadn't quite put the face and the name together. He is the son of Dan Cantor, a longtime regular at the morning minyan at Stanton Street, and he is also the father of Noah Cantor, whom I may or may not have ever met but who was reported by a mutual friend, an academic colleague, to have thoroughly approved of my old article, "Voices around the Text," about MTJ as it was in the 1980s.

Such multigenerational East Siders might still, without too much of a stretch, be considered the "core" of the Orthodox community, but they are all too aware that they are not reproducing themselves and that the community's institutions are dwindling in turn. One day in late 2013, I overheard Yisroel Ruven deep in conversation with Yitzkhok Sperber, owner of the kosher grocery store, and Mickey Schwartz, a longtimer at the Bialystoker Synagogue near Grand Street who was one of the plaintiffs in a lawsuit against the rabbi and the board arising out of the recent sale of the Orenstein Building, a residence for the elderly next to that synagogue. They were evidently discussing an upcoming vote of the membership of the Bialystoker Shul and the difficulty of arranging for a majority of local (resident) member votes in order to block another sale, this time of the parcel of land immediately north of the Bialystoker Shul. They were also discussing whether the Rosh Yeshiva would stay in the neighborhood "if there aren't any more stores." The prospect of the Rosh Yeshiva's leaving was thus tightly linked to the neighborhood's prospective disappearance as an organized Orthodox Jewish community.

Later, as Yisroel Ruven and his current study partner were sitting down to study, he wanted to talk about it a bit more, or maybe I prompted him. "You were there for the Eighth Street Shul" (which was sold without consulting or obtaining the consent of the congregation in the 1990s), "you know what happens in a dying neighborhood. It used to happen all the time—look at all the shuls that are gone." Yisroel Ruven pointed out to me that as part of this deal the building housing Rabbi Karp's shul—that is, the nursing home known as the Home of the Sages of Israel—would come down, too. The Bialystoker Shul would get twenty million dollars out of the deal.

"And what are they going to do with it?" I asked.

"That's just it," replied Yisroel Ruven. "There's nothing they can do with it. That money's restricted," that is, the proceeds of this sale by a nonprofit could only be put to certain not-for-profit uses. Yisroel Ruven thought the only way the deal could be stopped was if the Rosh Yeshiva became involved, "and that's not likely to happen. It'll only happen if Yitzkhok Sperber convinces him. Me, I'm like his son [so he wouldn't listen to me] but Yitzkhok Sperber is a *malach* [an angel]." However, Yisroel Ruven is not necessarily opposed to the sale of any of these buildings under any circumstances. What he is clear about, consistent with rulings of the Rosh Yeshiva and the Rosh Yeshiva's father before him, is that the proceeds of the sale of any communal assets remain in the community, to be used for purposes such as housing for Orthodox Jewish families.

About a year and a half later, I went to the yeshiva for the Sabbath afternoon services, which I had been enjoying partly because on that day, unlike the weekdays, the Rosh Yeshiva would sit and study at his desk in the beis medresh. He wasn't there that afternoon, however, and Yisroel Ruven told me he hadn't been coming in on Sabbath afternoons: "He's getting old." He asked me if I'd been to the early Bialystoker minyan, and then if there were any "fireworks this week."

I replied, "No, why?"

Yisroel Ruven replied that the previous week there had been a big fight. The president and three of the board members had resigned. "They realize there's trouble [over the land deal] and they don't want to be in any deeper." And he told me that two more Jewish Lower East Side institutions were on their way out: the funeral home on East Broadway known as Adas Yisroel had been sold ("there's scaffolding there already"); and the *nayn-un-nayntsiger* (a synagogue so called because its congregation had once been located at number 99, but on a totally different street) had been sold by a board of Lakewood, New Jersey, residents who lived on the Lower East Side as kids, and wanted to recreate the minyan down there. I mentioned the deal for the Home of the Sages of Israel, and Yisroel Ruven said, "He [the person who engineered the sale] could have saved himself a lot of trouble if he'd given even a little bit of the money to the neighborhood—$100,000 to the yeshiva, some more to the Bialystoker, and nobody would have said boo. I can understand if the people running these places aren't *frum* [observant] Jews, but frum Jews should understand that the money has to go back to the community."

One day as we waited for the shiur to start, the same theme came up in connection with another lost neighborhood institution. "That guy from Geneva who comes in—he has a lot of money, right?"

"Yeah, he's talking about buying the lumber yard [across the street] and expanding the yeshiva."

"Why not just build in the backyard here?"

"That's worth about $4,000,000."

This speculation about the value of various parcels of real estate brought the conversation to the topic of the recently collapsed and sold Roumanian Synagogue on Rivington Street.

Sure, they [sons of the rabbi who maintained the shul in its last decades] wanted it to fall down so it would be easier to sell. Originally it was zoned for eleven floors and they were going to get $12,000,000 for it; now it's down to nine so they're just getting $9,000,000. The Rosh Yeshiva said that when any communal property in the neighborhood is sold, the proceeds should stay in the neighborhood [donated to a Jewish charitable cause locally]. Not that it should be spent on trips to Israel to look for Torah scrolls or to decide what tzedakah [charity] to give it to there. And [the family that controls the Beis Medresh Hagadol on Norfolk Street, which at that time was landmarked] are just waiting for it to fall down too, because then politically it's easier to just sell it.[3]

Neighborhood Watch

Still, the community is sufficiently intact that its members can keep tabs on each other as we go about our rounds. One afternoon I had left the yeshiva and waited outside the Café Grumpy on Essex Street north of Canal, waiting for Elissa's cousin Neil so we could have our regular Thursday afternoon city walk. I took out my tuna sandwich and started eating. Howard Mandelbaum, a regular at the yeshiva who would be working out of town as a Hillel rabbi if he could get the position, passed by and said, "Even though you're eating in the street, you're still not *posul far eydes* [ineligible to give testimony in a Jewish court]." In the times of the Talmud, this was such outlandish behavior that the rabbis ruled one who did so an unreliable witness, but Howard told me, "Rabbi Avigdor Miller [of the Brooklyn Orthodox community] says that since lots of people do it now, you can eat in the street and still be a witness."

One night, Elissa attended a community board meeting, dealing with the application for permanent recognition of her community garden across the street from the Stanton Street Shul. As we sat and waited for the Rosh Yeshiva the next day, Yisroel Ruven's uncle, a regular member of the shiur, told us that he had left a meeting (although he didn't tell us what the meeting was about) and encountered a demonstration protesting the decision not to indict the policeman who shot a young black man named Michael Brown in Ferguson, Missouri. "They were shouting, 'Hands up, don't shoot!' What does that have to do with it?"

I asked him if he was a member of the community board, and when he told me he was, I mentioned that my wife had been at the meeting as well. He asked her name, I told him, and he rolled his eyes and said, "I'm not going to say anything." But he couldn't quite restrain himself and added, "She should ask *daas Torah* [here, meaning a rabbinical opinion] before she gets up to speak at a community board meeting. And as far as I'm concerned, it doesn't have to be from here. She can shop around. But she should have some rabbinic authority on her side before she gets up and says things in public." He didn't say what issue he was referring to and I didn't ask, but I'm almost certain it was the then-pending application for landmarking of the Bialystoker Home for the Aged on East Broadway (*not* the Home of the Sages of Israel, *not* the Bialystoker Shul, but yet another neighborhood institution that had been closed down and was then threatened with demolition, though it has since been landmarked).

I learn about others with a longtime connection to the neighborhood because I myself have been here almost forty years. Shortly after I started coming to the yeshiva, an older man who regularly studies at the next table from us, carrying on deliberations over the text in a rich native Yiddish, came and introduced himself as Simcha Fiedler. "Where are you from?"

"East Third Street and Avenue A."

"I used to manage the First Houses" (across the street from our apartment building, and so named because they were the first public housing in the United States, in 1934).

"Where do you daven?" he asked further.

I told him, "Stanton Street."

He responded, "Oh, Rabbi Singer's shul." That was precisely right—we always called it "Rabbi Singer's shul," rather than the Stanton Street Shul, when the European-born Rabbi Singer was still there.

"Is there anybody left there?"

"A few people," I replied, "but my wife and I are the older generation now."

Kosher Enough?

Here's a short story about my own confusion. One Friday, the day after the holiday of Shevuos, I was in the yeshiva for an hour following the funeral of the man I called Pete Silver in *Mornings at the Stanton Street Shul*. At minchah, Rabbi Brody, the principal of the school for boys from kindergarten through high school, said he'd heard I was giving the *kiddush* (refreshments after the service) at Bialystok the next morning and asked if I'd ordered from Usher, a local hasidic caterer. I said no, I'd ordered from "Yitzkhok." Now Rabbi Yitzkhok Sperber, very respected at the yeshiva, runs the grocery store on Grand Street, and I remembered (or thought I remembered) that the Stanton Street Shul where I've also been a member for decades orders prepared food for the kiddush from the grocery store. And I knew that the Rosh Yeshiva's brother, the head of the flourishing branch of MTJ called the Yeshiva of Staten Island, but at that time still living on the Lower East Side, would only eat when the kiddush food is catered by Usher. When I had gone in to pay for the kiddush at the Bialystok office, the secretary asked whether I wanted to get the food from Usher or . . . she may have said Yitzy, not Yitzkhok . . . and I probably said Yitzkhok. Knowing that the Rosh Yeshiva's brother wouldn't be there that week anyway, I chose to go with the latter, even though some may consider Usher's food more reliably kosher.

It turned out that whoever "Yitzy" is, he's not the owner of the grocery store, but an entirely different caterer who doesn't live in the neighborhood, as Rabbi Brody explained: "He was fired from the butcher and there are reasons for that. He lives in Borough Park. And there's no *hashgachah* [kosher supervision] on his food, so you just have to trust him. The rabbi at Bialystok says we have no reason to doubt his kashrut, so we can't stop people from ordering from him. But the Silverblatt brothers [longtime regulars at the early Sabbath services at Bialystok] are the only ones who order from Yitzy." Seeing that he had upset me, he backed off: "You had no way of knowing," and generally retreated from the suggestion that Yitzy's food isn't kosher.

When I saw him in shul the next morning, he was very friendly, to the extent of making the extraordinary gesture of kissing his finger after shaking my hand—a gesture that we've learned from some of the Mediterranean Jews but certainly hasn't become common in the yeshiva world. And the day after that we had the following e-mail exchange, partially prompted by my desire to show there were no hurt feelings on my part:

> Dear Rabbi Brody,
>
> As I mentioned in shul this morning, I'm writing to let you know about the *chesed shel emes* [altruistic kindness] performed by seven of your MTJ high school boys at the funeral for our neighbor and friend Pete Silver on Friday. Pete's father, Dan Silver, was a leading supporter of MTJ, remembered by some who are still there such as Rabbi Karp. The *bokhurim* made their way promptly to Montefiore Cemetery at Rabbi Andy Licht's call, participated actively in the *levaye* [funeral] and made it possible for a *kaddish* [memorial prayer] to be said at the graveside.
>
> Their act speaks well of MTJ under your stewardship.
>
> *a gut vokh* [a good week],
>
> Jonathan Boyarin

He replied:

> I showed ur email to the r yeshiva & r Nobel. Both were appreciative of ur kind words. Btw I'm sorry if I caused u anguish concerning ur kind gesture at ur kiddish yesterday. U had no way of knowing.

And I replied in turn:

> Please don't worry about that—I'm sorry there are these 'fault lines' in the community but I'm an anthropologist and I know that's how communities work in the real world.

In short, my "revenge" was getting to suggest to him that there may be some value to the community in my being an anthropologist.

What's Not Kosher This Month?

Regulars at MTJ are also well aware that standards in the yeshivish Orthodox world around them have shifted with respect to issues such as kashrut standards and gender separation. Some observers would characterize this as a shift to the right. Others would counter that greater knowledge of the law and an increase in personal piety have led to more precise adherence to Jewish law.

One day a group of rabbis came in shortly after 1:00 p.m. and waited for the Rosh Yeshiva to finish minchah. He had arranged a meeting with them, and actually cancelled his 2:00 p.m. shiur. Later I learned that the meeting concerned a potential problem that had come up with the kashrut of grapes. Evidently a larger number of bugs than usual had been detected in Chilean grapes, and the question was whether they are on the surface (and thus could potentially be washed off) or infest the inside of the fruit. I learned these details when someone (Nasanel? Yisroel Ruven?) approached Rabbi Karp to ask whether the results of the meeting were known yet, and I overheard: "But people have to eat grapes!"

As we prepared the next day, Yisroel Ruven offered each of us—Asher, Hillel, and me—a choice of a mini Mars bar or Snickers, amid banter about grapes. I mentioned that I'd been to a reception the previous evening, and I had eaten a lot of grapes. (While I was eating them, in fact, I wasn't thinking about the halachic question at all.) I never did hear clearly about the outcome of the previous day's meeting, but my guess was that the Rosh Yeshiva hadn't agreed to declare that grapes are now unkosher, since when someone jokingly asked what the Rosh Yeshiva would do when Yisroel Ruven gave him a bunch of grapes, Yisroel Ruven said, "He'll wash them off and eat them." Meanwhile, the little candies gave Asher a chance to joke, "With the candy, now we just need some salmon,[4] grapes, and tap water. We know already the tap water is no good.[5] Just look on the door of the yeshiva—it's the Rosh Yeshiva's only published *teshuva* [response to a particular question in Jewish law]."

Other Shuls, Other Jews

There's an old joke: the person to the right of me is a fanatic, and the person to the left of me is a heretic. In a neighborhood whose Jewish population has been declining for roughly a century, and where buildings to house Jewish institutions have been progressively emptied out, the narcissism of small differences bears a particular pathos. Overall MTJ remains a bastion against gestures toward change in synagogue practice, especially the expansion of women's ritual roles. My synagogue on Stanton Street is the standard-bearer for those changes on the Lower East Side. Some at MTJ seem to be bothered by this, others not.

One evening early in my kollel year, as I was heading out, one of the regulars wished me a good night, and asked whether I live in Brooklyn.

"No, here, on Third Street."

"Third Street? You got [the] Stanton Street [Shul] and Chasam Sopher there."

"Yeah, we go to Stanton Street."

"Oh, I know the *baal koyre* [Torah reader] there, he's very good."

On the other hand, a few days earlier, we had entered the library one morning to find a smaller group gathered for the Rosh Yeshiva's shiur than usual, perhaps because of the traffic occasioned by the victory parade for the Super Bowl–winning Giants downtown. As we were waiting for the Rosh Yeshiva to come in, Asher addressed me directly, but not quite privately: "I saw posters up for the Stanton . . . they have a women's minyan?"

"Yeah, a few times a year."

"Who *layens* [reads the Torah]?"

"There are several women who know how."

"There's a rabbi there?"

"The rabbi's upstairs, but of course he approved it."

After a pause, Asher responded: "That's one thing they never had on the East Side, is a Conservative or Reform shul." These more liberal denominations have been far more willing than Orthodox synagogues to grant women equal ritual roles. Whether he meant further to imply that the changes I was attesting to at Stanton Street actually constitute evidence of a slide toward non-Orthodoxy, I cannot say.

Too Religious?

Yisroel Ruven, for one, feels free to poke at tendencies toward a *farfrumt*, overly restrictive, version of contemporary Orthodox Judaism. One day it came up that a shiur member's wife doesn't sit with him at the same table when they eat. "What, you don't even sit with your wife in the house?" responded Yisroel Ruven with open incredulity. "That's crazy!"

Another time I heard Yisroel Ruven complain about the spreading practice, under the influence of contemporary Hasidism, of separate seating for men and women at communal events. He took the occasion to recall the funeral of the deeply beloved previous Mashgiach, whom I had known in the 1980s: "At the Mashgiach's funeral, they stretched out the curtain [in the beis medresh] that separates the women's section over there. Rabbi Nobel put it back up, and said, 'This is not our minhag!'" Yet, he continued, at a bris (circumcision) celebrated downstairs in the lunchroom just recently, the men and women had sat separately.

Yet another trait associated with Hasidism, and more broadly with a greater separatism from the general culture, is belief in the efficacy of certain formulas or ritual objects to help one get what he wishes for. This belief is another of Yisroel Ruven's targets, since in his loyalty to the ethos of the yeshiva he bristles at the influence Hasidim are perceived to have over what was once a more distinct and overtly antihasidic, Lithuanian yeshiva world. One day— unprovoked by anything that I could determine, other than the fact that it was a Tuesday—Yisroel Ruven announced, in mock solemn tones, "*Rabosay*, 160 years ago Reb Mendel of Rimenev announced that anyone who says [a certain Psalm] on Tuesday will become rich. And if he doesn't become rich," added Yisroel Ruven as his own commentary, "at least he'll be a *baal betochen* [a true believer]."

Rabbi Pinsker responded: "It can't hurt, can it?"

And Yisroel Ruven insisted, "It's a waste of time!" Citing authority in support of his implicit claim that such beliefs in what might be termed superstitious or magical techniques is a deviation from true Judaism, Yisroel Ruven added: "As the Rosh Yeshiva says [disparagingly], *am segulos*"—a people of amulets, a takeoff of the phrase *am segula*, which is generally but problematically glossed as "chosen people."

One morning when I came in, Hillel, Asher, and a fellow named Azriel Meir were discussing the meaning of *tsnius*, a word generally translated as "modesty" but also implying humility, as in the prophet's adjuration to "walk humbly with your God" (Micah 6:8). In everyday parlance, the term is used primarily to refer to standards of women's behavior. Hillel told an anecdote about two secular Israeli women going door to door selling cosmetics. A religious woman answers, and then says she can't let them in because her husband is at home learning and they're not dressed appropriately. The secular women retort, "We're not dressing to show off. We go out dressed this way because we're comfortable this way. Haredi women dress up and put on lots of cosmetics just to go to the store!" Hillel was evidently sympathetic to the position of the secular women in this anecdote, not because he thought they should set the standard but because he thinks women dressing to be attractive to men is inherently a violation of tsnius. Azriel Meir wants to hew much closer to the definition of tsnius as focusing on sexual modesty, nonexhibitionism. Asher, chiming in at the end, insisted that tsnius means a woman dresses respectably but not to impress anybody else, including her friends—and he quoted the *Chofetz chaim* in approving tones to the effect that this might be a woman's highest mitzvah, the most sacred thing she can attend to.

Litvaks and Hasidim

As Elissa reminds me, the Stanton Street Shul, in the northern part of the Lower East Side, is where Jews from the Austro-Hungarian province of Galicia, who were primarily hasidic, settled. The lower part, around Grand Street, was more "Litvak"—here meaning not just those from the region that was Lithuania between the two world wars, but the extended region of the Polish-Lithuanian Commonwealth as early as the sixteenth century. For some at MTJ, relearning how to be a true "Litvak" is part of the training. One day I came in to hear the continuation of a discussion whose first part I had evidently missed. In a conversation with Yisroel Ruven and Eli, Hillel had strenuously denied feeling the *kedusha*, the holiness of the Land of Israel, when he was there. Yisroel Ruven purported to be very upset by Hillel's views on this topic, although (as usual) without any rancor. In the brief ensuing discussion, Hillel insisted he was working on developing his rationalist, antihasidic persona. Then he tried to convince Yisroel Ruven to consider the difference between his own emotions when Yisroel Ruven is in Israel, and the sanctity of the land itself, as a putative external source of those emotions. Was Yisroel Ruven making himself feel like he was on holy ground, or was he feeling the holiness?

"It's not important for me to know that!" Yisroel Ruven insisted. "It's important to have the feelings." This time, even though Hillel purported to be consciously striving to maintain a Litvak sensibility, the result he arrived at was not one that Yisroel Ruven could endorse.

Nevertheless, part of what was at stake in this exchange seemed to be a contest over who's the real rationalist Jew, the real Misnagid. As in the examples above, Yisroel Ruven wants to uphold a reasonable Orthodoxy against a perceived wave of increasing stringency, much of which might be attributed to the influence of contemporary hasidic communities. Here, his insistence that performance—*even the performance of experience of emotion*—is more important than interiority or proper "intent" seems to reflect that same sensibility. At the same time, Hillel is insisting that it's wrong to be deluded by popular ideologies into misreading one's own experience. He, too, clearly understands this as tied to his commitment to a nonhasidic, "Litvak" tradition, for he insists that he rejects even some hasidic customs that his father (a pulpit rabbi) practices. And thus the occasion presented itself for Yisroel Ruven and Asher to tease him again about the fact that, as a young child, Hillel himself underwent the hasidic ceremony of *upshern*, the first haircut that (at about the age of three) initiates the hasidic boy into the first stages of formal education. Hillel played his part well, purporting to be embarrassed in turn by the reminder. How genuinely it distressed him I could not say, but the exchange proved to be the occasion for another pop-culture reference. When Hillel got up for a second, Yisroel Ruven commented on Hillel's provocateur stance: "He's trying to be another Sacha Baron Cohen."

Part of the "Litvak" ethos, closely linked to a vaunted emphasis on scholarship, is an insistence on being able to articulate the basis on Jewish law for following or disallowing a specific practice. (From another perspective, one might say that a common strategy is to deny that a specific practice of which one disapproves has or could have an identifiable basis in Jewish law.) One winter afternoon I went to spend the last hours of Shabbes at MTJ. Yisroel Ruven was there, relaxed, and I had an opportunity to chat with him and others. As I sat down to join them for the meal, I realized that Yisroel Ruven was complaining about some practice that he doesn't believe is based in legitimate sources. "Show me a *Mishnah berurah* or an *Aruch hashulchan*[6] that talks about it."

I asked him what he was talking about, and he explained that it was the hasidic custom of celebrating the last day of Chanukah as "the Feast of Messiah." This led him to general unflattering remarks about Hasidim: "Yeah, I don't like them, because when I'm in the country, the *goy* doesn't want to deal with me because he's just had to deal with eighty Hasidim." The only Hasidim he respects, he said, are those from the Gerer community, because they take learning seriously and don't talk while they're davening.

The younger men present teased him that he had hasidic tendencies when he was younger, which he tried to deny.

I put in, "Only somebody with a *shemets* [trace or hint] of *khsides* [Hasidism] would talk about them in such a *farbisn* [bitter] way," and the joke was appreciated.

I mentioned to Yisroel Ruven that a few years ago, I had asked somebody from Williamsburg whether there's a tzaddik (saint) there.

"I'll show you a tzaddik from Williamsburg. Do you know Rabbi Feffer? Did you know Avrom Feffer?"

"Yeah," I replied. Avrom Feffer was a great and troubled character whom I used to know in the 1980s. He was the source of one of my best Jewish one-liners, which he shouted to the whole beis medresh one day in the mid-1980s, apropos of nothing that I could determine at the time or later. It was a comment on the prevalent use of the term *frum* or, depending on one's dialect, *frim*, to designate observant Jews: "Frim! A galekh iz frim! A yid iz erlekh!" (Pious! A Christian priest is pious! A Jew is honest!)

"Rabbi Feffer is Avrom's father—he's been the first-grade rebbi here for about fifty years."

I took the opportunity to ask Yisroel Ruven what sort of Hasidim Rabbis Feld and Schuster are. Their presence at MTJ for decades as fully respected members of the learning community adequately testifies that however sensitive some at the beis medresh may be to the need to maintain a Litvak sensibility, Hasidim have long been welcome there. In any case, Yisroel Ruven told me that "Schuster is from that group upstate, past Yonkers."

"Nitra," I say.

"Yeah, Nitra. And Mendl Feld is a *baal teshuva* [usually, a Jew who has become observant or returned to observance, but here used jokingly]. He was a Chaim Berlin [one of the major New York Lithuanian-style yeshivas] guy who married a Satmar [hasidic] girl, and joined them. And he's raised his kids very successfully in Satmar, they're completely . . ."

"Integrated."

"Yeah, integrated."

"And he seems to fit in very well there, too."

"Yeah, he does, but not many Satmar guys know Carlebach tunes."

All of this suggests that some of Feld's slightly self-parodying performance as a Hasid, such as when he sets a summertime lunch of leftovers before us with the announcement "Raboysay, s'i du veg-e-tab-les!" (Gentlemen, there are vegetables!), comes from his knowing stance as an outsider/insider.

Some glimpses of the future of this tension about retaining a distinction between yeshivish and hasidic worlds can be obtained through eavesdropping on the conversation of the younger boys. Another Shabbes afternoon, I'd overheard a couple of the young bar-mitzvah age boys kibitzing; perhaps there were more of them present than usual because that morning, there had been a bar mitzvah at the yeshiva. Though I didn't catch much detail, the conversation certainly seemed to be about where the boundaries should be between "us" and "them," and I heard one blond kid saying, "Yeah, [you'll marry a hasidic woman and] twenty years from now you'll wake up and say, 'How come my wife is bald?'" He was referring to the hasidic practice of having women shave their heads at marriage, rather than merely wear a wig or otherwise cover their hair in public. Evidently "even" at this preteen level, the boys were well aware of the tendencies toward adoption of hasidic stringencies.

After the *shales sudes* ritual meal that afternoon, as I was sitting and learning by myself, the same blond kid sat across from me and opened the conversation with, "So how do you like learning with [Nasanel] Schoenstein?"

I told him that basically I liked it very much, although it can be frustrating because it's hard to get Nasanel to stick to the text. He went on to ask me where I live when I'm not in New York, and then was very curious about what I teach. I told him that Jewish studies includes things like Jewish history, "but also the same kind of stuff we learn in here. Only of course it's approached very differently. For instance, it's not just for Jews." I told him, for dramatic effect, that there's a non-Jewish woman who's a full professor of Talmud at an Ivy League university.

He was fascinated: "And she knows how to read Rashi, too?" I assured him that she indeed knows how to read Rashi. He wanted to know more about Cornell: Is it Ivy League? Does it have a law school? What's it like to try to be frum there? I love this kid, a bit of a wise guy but not obnoxious, totally East Side, smart and wanting to learn about the world.

Politics

Electoral politics—especially, but not only at the national level in the United States—are one of the common topics of casual conversation during breaks from intense study. Over the years spanning the second election of Barack Obama, the election of Donald Trump, and well into Trump's presidency, these conversations seemed to presume a consensus in favor of more conservative and usually Republican candidates. Indeed, surveys generally show that while American Jews as a whole tend to vote as liberals, Orthodox Jews are more at the conservative end of the spectrum. At times I'm still puzzled about the exact process by which a right-wing attitude toward general American politics became normative in this community.

One day there was a discussion, mostly carried out by Max Greenberg, with Asher and Hillel as semiwilling audience, begun before the shiur and continued after. The halachic question posed had to do with menstrual taboos, and with the related cyclical preparations for approved marital sex. As Max phrased it: "Do we advise a single woman to go to the mikvah [ritual bath]?" and thus purify herself after menstruation, if we know that she is sleeping with Jewish men, even though not married. In other words, do we

advise her to fulfill this commandment even though we understand that in her case, it is a preparation for behavior that is not
condoned.

The answer: "No, because there must be standards," and so we
wouldn't want to provide a halachic cover for behavior that is
deemed grossly immodest. Max contrasted this to listening to the
radio (presumably chosen because it is also less than an ideal practice, but less flagrant than sex between two unmarried Jews). Here,
he argued, the appropriate answer to a question about its permissibility might be: "Instead of doing what?" The implied message
was that listening to the radio might be deemed a "harmless" activity and a better alternative than more provocative or distracting
secular stimuli, or, in another context, might be deemed a distraction from the study of Torah or the observance of other mitzvos.
To specify, he added, "I don't mean dirty radio—I mean something like Rush Limbaugh or Sean Hannity."

Another day in early November 2012, I joined Asher for the first
time since Hurricane Sandy, a bit earlier in the morning since before that interruption, Asher had taken up my suggestion that we
start preparing at 9:45 a.m. instead of at 10:15 a.m. I didn't encourage chat about the storm, even though I was very curious to know
how it had been weathered at the yeshiva. However, Asher felt
moved to say a word about the election. "Boy, I hope Romney gets
elected." Like Max, he appeared to assume that I was as worried at
the prospect of Obama's reelection as he was.

I chose not to enter into a discussion about national politics.
While I suspect that the range of intellectual freedom that I sense
at MTJ would extend to a well-articulated defense of a more liberal view than seems to be the consensus there, something about
my personality or my situation led me to avoid taking the bait and
starting that argument. Much as I would like those whom I respect
at MTJ to share my views on these "outside" issues, I have never
been moved to try to persuade them. Instead, I gave an ambiguous
answer that didn't quite endorse Asher's worries, but gave him
room for them: "Well, it seems awfully close." In fact, I too was

anxious about the outcome, though my anxiety was different from Asher's.

Asher remarked how calm the Rosh Yeshiva seems to be about such things: "When Obama was elected, one of the guys went up to the Rosh Yeshiva and he was almost crying, 'What's going to be, Rebbi?' But the Rosh Yeshiva was calm about it."

I said nothing further, and Asher concluded the political discussion by saying, "Well, if it's a *zchus* [merit] for the Jewish people that Romney gets elected, he should get elected."

To which I replied, "Amen." I didn't think it likely that in the long run, a Romney presidency would turn out to be good for the Jews—but who knows?

And then just two days after Obama was reelected, Asher told me how hard it had been for him to get home to Brooklyn the evening before, due to continued disruption of subway service in the wake of Hurricane Sandy and the nor'easter the previous night. "The F train stopped at Church Avenue, one stop before mine. The conductor announced, 'Everybody off, this train's going out of service.' So I found the Mashgiach, and we got a bus, and the bus took us a few blocks, and then we walked. . . . I told the Mashgiach what the Rosh Yeshiva had said the last time Obama was elected, and he said, 'He is very optimistic.'"

In most of these conversations, a conservative stance toward secular politics seems to be a given, something that just goes along naturally with being a member of the Orthodox community. There are a number of reasons for this. One is the perceived association between liberalism and unconventional sexual mores, and more generally with individual choice of mate as opposed to conformity with communal standards. Another has to do with an urban history in which liberalism is linked to the battle over African Americans' civil rights and thus to a perceived threat to the security of Jewish communities. A third is the perceived anti-Zionism of what remains of the "Left," often conflated with antisemitism. Rarely are these attitudes explicitly grounded in a "Torah perspective," although the twentieth century provides plenty of evidence for suppression of Orthodox Judaism by east European Communists in power.

Occasionally, however, opinions on these more general political issues were tied to larger principles or more long-standing historical patterns. This was especially true for Nasanel, a wide-ranging, speculative intellectual who works hard to make connections between what are for most people disparate realms of discourse and concern. One day after the Gemara shiur, he found himself torn between studying with me in the beis medresh and standing near the Rosh Yeshiva's door to wait his turn for an audience. The eventual compromise was to bring my copy of the *Tur* to the hallway next to the Rosh Yeshiva's office, where Nasanel, in his usual loud voice, continued on the theme of the morality of mass slaughter and the divine right of kings. Effi Kliger came by to remind Nasanel that the Rosh Yeshiva can hear him from inside his office. Then it was time for me to go; I had schoolwork to do, I had to get back to Ithaca the next day, and I had a cold. Nasanel walked me home, as far as Houston Street, where I sent him back to the yeshiva. All the way he talked about the principle of the divine right of kings—its origins, its scope, and to what extent belief in the principle was a matter of consensus among Jewish thinkers. He wondered whether this kind of privilege properly extends to a dictator, or even a popularly elected president: "True, the Abarbanel[7] preferred republics to kingdoms, but he was an exception in that, and he had suffered greatly at the hands of King Ferdinand."

Outside Influences

Although total concentration on Torah to the exclusion of secular phenomena might be occasionally praised at MTJ, there's little effort on anyone's part to pretend that he hasn't been exposed to the wider world of either secular Jewish or Gentile culture—or in some cases, even to more critical or historical strands within Jewish scholarship. To be sure, such strictures as there are might be too much for some. Henoch, a young unmarried man who was spending a couple of years in yeshiva before moving on and marrying, bent my ear for a bit, because he'd realized that he can talk about his marginally appropriate ideas safely with me. He'd discovered that the Hertz Bible, written by the chief rabbi of the British Empire early in the twentieth century, had preempted his idea of a Bible translation that would stress the moral issues. Henoch said, "They [yeshivish people] don't like Hertz because he challenged Wellhausen," that is, he explicitly took issue with the rather antisemitic nineteenth-century German scholar Julius Wellhausen, known as the founder of source criticism. As a result, anyone who looks at Hertz's edition of the Pentateuch will be exposed to the notion of source criticism. "In their [yeshivish] view, we shouldn't be talking about Wellhausen at all."

The fastest-growing and most readily available source of "outside" information during the years I recall in this book has, of course, been the Internet. Unlike some other segments of the traditionalist Orthodox world, the Internet does not seem to be regarded as a source of inherent and unmitigated evil at MTJ. One day in the Gemara shiur, the Rosh Yeshiva puzzled over a comment in Tosafos that refers to a possible *gezera shava*, a hermeneutic derivation from the appearance of the same word in two different scriptural contexts, this one based on two appearances of the word *alah* (upon it). "So he [Tosafos] talks about a *gezera shava alah alah* [a derivation from the law that pertains to one appearance of the word *alah* to the second context in which *alah* appears], but I have no idea where he got it. Today, with the internet, you could search for *alah alah* and find it in two seconds." I don't think he was suggesting anyone should do it, although there were several people present at the shiur who might have been able to attempt this Google search on their phones. It's the kind of information the Rosh Yeshiva generally treats as potentially valid, but nevertheless something we can live without if it's not readily present in our books.

Prime Directive

One afternoon right after the Gemara shiur, Nasanel chose to spend twenty minutes talking at me, starting from a question I had about the Gemara's reading of the tannaitic text. He pointed to a passage earlier in Bava Kama that declares that the "Jerusalemites" (that is, the Tannaim for the most part) speak "loosely." In the course of Nasanel's explanation of the "loose" speech of the Tannaim, he used the word "cadre," placing the accent on the second syllable. Doubtless this is a word he's read several times but never heard pronounced—I have made the same mistake with talmudic terms and been gently corrected by Nasanel in turn. (A few days earlier, he had been talking about "King Croesus," with the first syllable being a long "o," and seemed genuinely distressed when I told him the whole world pronounces that name "Krieses.")

I corrected him gently, as always: "Most people pronounce that word 'cadre'" (with the accent on the first syllable). Then I wanted to explain further my hesitation to correct him (explaining further is never a faux pas with Nasanel, who explains endlessly what's on his mind): "Do you know about the Prime Directive on Star Trek?"

Nasanel responded with a detailed account of the genesis of the Prime Directive, stemming from episodes where the Klingons had helped one side of a civil war with advanced weapons, and Captain Kirk had decided to even out the odds by giving weapons to the other side, with disastrous consequences all around: "So Starfleet Command issued the Prime Directive, which was not to interfere with the internal development of alien civilizations. It makes sense when you don't have the ability to exercise superb judgment, but when you do, it's appropriate to interfere."

After Nasanel rehearsed the Prime Directive in much more detail than I could have provided, I explained to him that I follow a version of the Prime Directive as an anthropologist, and am hence torn whether to correct him or not on these unusual pronunciations—the main thing, I told him, is that I don't want him to feel patronized. "So if you don't want me to correct you, I won't."

He allowed me to do so, feigning reluctance and asserting, in turn, that he deliberately uses these mispronunciations as a diagnostic: if people aren't taking him seriously after hearing these mispronunciations, he knows that they're not sincere in turn. Then he came upon a happy solution: "I'll say 'Krieses' to everybody else but 'Krosus' to you."

Practices and Wisdom of the Gentiles

One day late in 2013, I was wondering about the justification of the embalming of Joseph, who was "placed in a coffin in Egypt" at the end of the book of Genesis. The commentary in the Hertz Bible, which I referred to above as also containing a defense of revealed Torah against the source criticism founded by Julius Wellhausen, explains that his father Jacob had been embalmed (against Jewish law) only in order to preserve his body until it could be buried in Israel. Trying to consult further commentaries, I asked one of the older rabbis to help me with a brief citation from the Baal Haturim,[8] brought in the ArtScroll khumesh. He explained the Baal Haturim's comment to me: just as someone who eulogizes another will in turn be eulogized and someone who mourns for another will be mourned, so too we are told that Joseph was honored with embalming because he had had his father embalmed. Then he added: the nineteenth-century commentator Malbim, staunchly traditionalist, but known to have considerable knowledge of secular sciences, links the Egyptian custom of embalming to their belief in the afterlife; hence the necessity not only for an intact body but for household goods to be buried along with the corpse (as we know from archaeology). "So apparently the Malbim must have heard this from somewhere" (i.e., he was paying attention to sources outside the yeshiva world).

Our Rosh Yeshiva, too, does not shy away from observations that testify to his awareness of secular trends. One time, as we were struggling with Rashi's comment at Bava Kama 49a, discussing the value of an animal some time after it has been stolen: "It says she *appears* fatter, implying that she isn't really [fatter and more valuable—she just looks nicer]. Like apples. They make them look nice but they don't taste as good. The ugly ones taste better. [brief pause] Organic."

Sacrifice and Reward

Although rabbinic texts are replete with discussions of the sacrifices one must make in order to devote oneself to Torah study, and of the rewards especially in the World to Come for such devotion (primarily the opportunity to continue studying eternally, without deprivation or distraction), not very much discussion is devoted to such motivations inside the beis medresh. To be sure, things come up. One day late in 2013, for the first time I could remember, the Rosh Yeshiva stopped the shiur around 11:45 a.m., saying, "Well, we went over enough days, I'm not going to start something new now." This reference to the shiur's frequent overtime led Gavriel Pinsker to remark to Zach, a retired musician who regularly attended the shiur in those days: "That day we got stuck on the Tosafos [and consequently Gavriel was late getting out of the yeshiva to work], the elevator before me [at work] was full of people and it got stuck." Implicitly, he was drawing a link between putting extra time into Torah study, and avoiding a major inconvenience. If I'm interpreting his statement correctly, the operative concept here is that of *hashgacha pratis*, divine supervision of the individual's fate. Even in the Orthodox world, seeing the divine hand at work everywhere, and especially as an explanation of one's own good fortune, can be overdone, and Rabbi Pinsker did not explicitly invoke it here.

Still, it's never considered bad form to mention something that turned out well in the end, especially if it may have seemed like a sacrifice for the sake of Torah at the time. I have never closely inquired about the yeshiva's sources of institutional support, or about the financial arrangements of most of the men who spend a good deal of time at MTJ. Though it would be consistent with east European Jewish social patterns to have the families of adult students supported, at least for a term of years, by in-laws or their own parents, I do not know if that is the case for anyone at MTJ. In any case, some of them are older and retired from positions such as property management or kashrut supervision. Some are younger and still living at home. Some are married to women who work at professions such as speech therapy or social work, in addition to their household responsibilities (though such matters do not often come up in casual conservation, and indeed as a general rule, those at MTJ do not frequently praise, complain, or otherwise talk casually to each other about their wives). One is the rabbi of a congregation in Brooklyn. Rabbi Pinsker is a professor of accounting at a college in Manhattan, and arranges his teaching schedule to leave his mornings free to attend the Rosh Yeshiva's shiur. Rabbi Goldman teaches classes in Talmud and Jewish law at various colleges and universities in New York City during the fall and spring semesters. Some of those I call here "regulars" are formally registered at MTJ, and receive a modest monthly stipend. Nasanel mentioned to me in 2012 that his stipend check was seven hundred dollars a month; and Yisroel Ruven once said to me, "You have no idea how much we [kollel members] give up to be here." No one has to pay tuition or dues in order to study in the beis medresh at MTJ. There is an annual dinner for the yeshiva as a whole (focusing on the lower grades through high school) and another one for the kollel. I take as generous an ad as I can in the kollel dinner journal, but no one has ever pressed me for a contribution, nor has anyone ever suggested I should register and receive a stipend.

One day I entered the yeshiva after three weeks away, to find that two items I'd ordered were waiting for me. One was a *kitl*, a white gown worn on certain ritual occasions, obtained for me by one of our last independent Jewish ritual professionals on the Lower East Side, a venerable scribe whose father originally established a storefront business on Essex Street. I'd left forty-five dollars with Rabbi Karp for it, so that was taken care of. I'd also asked Rabbi Schuster to get me a copy of the commentary of the late medieval scholar known as Ritva on tractate Yevamos. (I was studying Yevamos, dealing with the rules of levirate marriage, with colleagues at Cornell.) This one I hadn't paid for before I left. Rabbi Schuster told me on the phone to give the money to Mendl Feld, "since we both live in Williamsburg."

I asked Rabbi Feld if he had change for a twenty-dollar bill, and he looked up at me in amused wonderment: *"Me?"*—as if to say, do you really think I have twenty dollars in my pocket?

Inevitably, there are conversations not only about how one can earn a living with a yeshiva background, but about the ways of making money that afford time to continue studying. One morning the chitchat before the shiur was about the advantages (you can make $50,000 in a day) and disadvantages (you can lose $50,000 in a day) of day-trading. Rabbi Pinsker mentioned that he had been a currency trader for some time, but retired from that work by thirty-five: "You have to have an iron stomach for that kind of work." Someone mentioned that 80 percent of commodity traders have ulcers, but someone else said that the people who go into that kind of work tend to be pretty hyper to begin with.

This brief anecdote suggests one material advantage being a full-time scholar at MTJ might have over more worldly pursuits: it is the cause of less anxiety. Other stories help clarify the various ways by which one achieves a place in the world of the yeshiva, decades ago or today. Asher told me about his great-uncle Joe, the youngest of three brothers (Asher's grandfather was the eldest) and the least scholarly, though he became a rabbi and had a congregation.

He had an entrance exam for [Yeshiva] Torah Vodaath [in Brooklyn]. I think it must have been in the '40s. And it was different then. You had to be really good, really serious to get in. So he comes in for the test, and the rebbi shows him a random passage, says, "Okay, look it over for half an hour, then I'll come in and talk to you about it."

Uncle Joe panicked: "How can I prepare this in half an hour?" Then he looked again, and he realized, "Oh, this is what I was learning with my brother yesterday!"

The rebbi comes in, and Uncle Joe explains the Gemara and the Rashi. The rebbi says, "I don't suppose you got to look at the Tosafos, too."

Uncle Joe starts talking about the Tosafos, and says, "And there's a [comment by the scholar know as] Maharsha on this . . ."

The rebbi interrupts him: "You're in!"

This story could be read in various ways. Perhaps most obviously, it seems to be another story about hashgacha pratis (again, divine providence), since Uncle Joe'ssubsequent career is here made to turn on the coincidence of being prepared for a very tough exam through the mere course of his regular study. It could also be taken as a comment on the seemingly arbitrary processes by which people obtain coveted and selective institutional slots, even though they may not seem to us more obviously worthy than those who do not. Or it could just be a funny story about someone who got "saved by the bell." To be sure, none of these readings is mutually exclusive, and if I am reluctant to overanalyze any of the stories I retell in this book, it is largely because I want to preserve intact the beauty of their multiple possible receptions.

Related both to the difficulty of earning a living and to the sacrifices entailed by a devotion to Torah study is the larger theme of exile: the perpetual tension of fealty to a system of obligations ultimately tied to sovereignty and homeland, in a situation of diaspora and coexistence with, if not outright domination by, non-Jewish Others. One week when the upcoming Torah potion was to narrate the beginning of the story of Jewish slavery in Egypt, the theme of the Mashgiach's mussar shmues was: "What is our function in *goles* [exile]?" He quoted midrashic accounts that describe God giving Abraham a choice of the form of penitence that the people Israel will undergo for their sins: either a period in Gehennom—just twelve months as a collective (in addition to whatever penance an individual may require), or subjugation to "the four kingdoms" (the successive empires of Egypt, Assyria, Babylon, and Rome). God advised Abraham to take earthly subjugation—the physical rather than the spiritual punishment— even though this would cause God pain, because God goes into exile with the people; and so Abraham did choose. The Mashgiach quoted the Maharal of Prague: just as God set the sun in its course and created all of the other forms and patterns of nature, so God gave each nation its proper land. Thus, exile is unnatural, a perversion of the order of nature. The world is not in order when Israel is in exile; it's as though the sun were to go backwards, or rain to fall up. On top of that, being in exile makes Israel sin even more, and that further lengthens the exile and further postpones the redemption. And if Abraham had not chosen the punishment of exile, we and our ancestors would all have been safe and sovereign in our land, where it's easy to follow the commandments of the Torah. Indeed, the Mashgiach concluded, because it is that much harder to keep the commandments and remain committed to Torah in exile, our accomplishments when we manage to do so are that much more precious.

Even though the argument acknowledged the desire to overcome exile and the congeniality of the Land of Israel for the observance of the commandments, I'm quite confident the Mashgiach did not mean to tell us that we should all be moving to Israel. While no one would be drummed out of the yeshiva for Zionism (contrast Hillel's experience at the Mir Yeshiva, described briefly in the previous chapter), neither is that ideology central or mandatory. Yisroel Ruven, for example, who had spent a fair amount of time studying in Israel, declared one day that he had no particular desire to go there again; he's had enough of it already.

Nor yet is there a consistent rejection of the pleasures of non-Jewish lands. As it happens, the Mashgiach himself is from

California. In another mussar shmues, he elaborated on a midrash that relates that Joseph obligated the Egyptians to circumcise themselves before he would give them food during the seven lean years. The shmues turned on the difference between the *yavonish* (Hellenistic) idea that males are born perfect with the foreskin, and the Jewish idea that circumcision is an amelioration. Later I approached him and told him: "My brother teaches in California, where there are a lot of people who are against circumcision."

"In San Francisco, probably," he answers.

"Probably. They say the parents are doing violence to their newborns. My brother says if our parents hadn't had us circumcised, that would have been a violence to us."

"Where's your brother—in Berkeley?"

"Yeah."

The Mashgiach: "That's the place to be! Only he's about four decades too late. They had a lot of fun there [back in the sixties]."

California dreamin' came up another time as well. Yisroel Ruven complained one morning that he wasn't getting enough sleep. "I'm still up at midnight—but you seem to be an early riser."

I replied, "Yeah, my kids are out of the house."

"How many kids?"

"Two boys."

"Where are they?"

"My older son's in San Francisco."

At which Asher interjected: "The weather's really nice in San Francisco, right? Maybe we should start a yeshiva there."

3

By Myself and with Others

LIKE OTHERS at MTJ, whether officially members of the kollel or
not, I find myself at various times studying on my own, in a pair,
in a small group, or in the context of a formal lesson. Almost anyone with extensive experience studying at other yeshivas would
find the patterns at MTJ less structured and more ad hoc than
most. The Rosh Yeshiva's daily shiurim and his Friday morning
shiur on the weekly Torah reading are, with the exception of the
Mashgiach's weekly half-hour mussar shmues, almost the only
regularly scheduled lessons, and even they are open to all but not
required.

Thus, the pattern of a day of study depends greatly on the individuals involved. My own routine has varied according to my level
of energy, how long I'm in town for, and the availability of others
to study with me, and I will not attempt to describe a "typical" day
of study here. Instead I will describe what it's like to study by myself, and then with some of the people you've already met. All of
these scenes of reading, whether solitary, cooperative, or hierar-
chical, center of course around a text that is not before us in *this*
book. Hence we will, as it were, repeatedly be looking over the
shoulders of readers, not quite being able to make out the little
black dots over which they puzzle, ourselves half comprehending
(and sometimes not even that) the moves by which they seek to
solve these puzzles.

Self-Study

When a newcomer enters the beis medresh planning to stay for a while, he is directed to Rabbi Karp, who counts among his various responsibilities doing what he can to make sure everyone who needs it is matched with a chevrusa. I didn't quite understand this when I walked in one day in December 2011 to begin what turned out to be my kollel year. I was looking for Simcha Goldman, since Rabbi Brody had told me he'd arranged for me to learn with Simcha. I spotted Rabbi Karp, asked for Simcha, and felt awkward when Rabbi Karp responded, "He's not here right now—are you looking for a chevrusa?" I politely refused what I took to be Rabbi Karp's offer to learn with him meanwhile instead. By a day or two later I had indeed met up with Simcha, and we studied together regularly for a few weeks, concentrating at my request on the sixteenth-century halachic code known as the *Arba turim*—my first experience studying legal digests rather than Talmud per se. In January, however, the local universities went back in session and Simcha resumed his routine of teaching extracurricular classes for students at several universities around New York City. Our study together has continued only sporadically since then.

A few months later I noted:

Without Simcha available for the 12:15–1:45 time slot, I felt a bit lost at the beginning of this week. I still feel awkward seeking Rabbi Karp's time, especially when it seems like he's to be a substitute. In any case, he wasn't ready for me the moment I left the Rosh Yeshiva's shiur, so I decided to spend whatever time between the Rosh Yeshiva's shiur and the moment Rabbi Karp signals that he's ready for me in "self-study." This is not unusual at the yeshiva; especially some of the younger men seem to spend a good part of the day studying on their own, yet it took at bit of time for me not to feel it like a deprivation. Even three or four weeks of studying the halachic codes with Rabbi Goldman has made it considerably more possible for me to do so on my own. So, perusing somewhat haphazardly a section of the *Tur*, my attention was caught by a phrase: "Where it's customary to eat the bread of Gentiles." And so I decided to study the laws pertaining to kosher bread.

It took me a while to find them. Although I asked Rabbi Karp where I would find that subject in the *Tur* and he told me clearly, chapter 112 in the volume known as *Yoreh de 'ah*, I couldn't find it at first: that's because I made the presumably common beginner's mistake of going to page 112 instead. Eventually I found the right page, and over the course of the week found the time to review, at least cursorily, the sources in the following order:

First, the Mishnah in Avodah Zarah (chapter 2, mishnah 5), which states flatly that the consumption of bread baked by non-Jews is forbidden;

Second, the Gemara there, which includes an anecdote that is the primary source for later debates about the permissibility of eating bread baked by a non-Jewish professional baker (but not in a Gentile's personal kitchen), and about the permissibility of eating Gentile bread "in the field" but not in town (since as all agree, the purpose of any restrictions on "Gentile" bread is quite explicitly the avoidance of the kind of cordial social relations that might lead to intermarriage);

Third, the *Tur* together with his major commentaries, the *Beis Yosef* (by Joseph Karo, who later distilled these discussions into the concise set of rules known as the *Shulchan aruch*), deemed presumptively authoritative since its publication in the sixteenth century, and the *Bach* (the *Bayis chadash*, or new house);

Fourth, the *Shulchan aruch* itself, from its writing until the present the foundational halachic authority for "Orthodox" Judaism,[1] although I haven't yet looked at its major commentaries, the *Shach* (*Sifsey cohen*, or lips of the priest) and the *Taz* (*Turei zahav*, or pillars of gold); and finally,

Aruch hashulchan, a late nineteenth-century work by Rabbi Yechiel Michel Epstein.

The *Tur* makes clear that, while a decree had been promulgated against eating the bread of a Gentile, this decree was not accepted in all Jewish communities. Hence his statement, "Where it's customary to eat Gentile bread." All of the authorities I looked at up to the *Aruch hashulchan* seem to agree that in any case, bread from a private Gentile's home may not be eaten, but the *Aruch hashulchan* argues that, on practical grounds, it's unreasonable to assume that every Jew has the option of baking his own bread (and thus can have bread while avoiding his neighbor's baking), and that, on textual grounds, all of the previous authorities had misread the Gemara when they read into it a complete ban on a private Gentile's bread even when no other bread was available. Perhaps, in fact, he was effectively providing a rationale for what many Jews living in small communities (where there was no professional baker at all) were already doing; but this raises the further question of how those isolated Jewish families could possibly make sure that their Gentile neighbor's ovens were kosher!

NOTICE: THE FOREGOING IS MERELY AN AUTOETH-NOGRAPHER'S REPORT ON HIS FIRST ATTEMPTS TO STUDY MATTERS OF JEWISH LAW ON HIS OWN, FROM THE ORIGINAL SOURCES. NO CONCLUSIONS ABOUT CURRENTLY EFFECTIVE JEWISH LAW SHOULD BE DRAWN THEREFROM. I am inspired in the wording of this caveat by an anecdote told me some time ago by a genial fellow congregant in the early Shabbes morning minyan at the Bialystoker Shul. "I used to have a Gemara teacher who was from Europe. We'd get through a *shtikl* [piece of] Gemara, and we'd say, 'Rebbi, what's the halacha?' And he'd say [in a heavy Yiddish accent], 'Ask your local Orthodox rabbi. Here, we're learning Gemara!'"

Of course, I'm neither an Orthodox rabbi nor a Gemara teacher. I'm an anthropologist and student. Yet, as these notes about my investigation of a certain halachic issue attest, after a few months I was already feeling somewhat less apologetic about my place in the yeshiva than I had the first couple of weeks. To be sure, it still made me uneasy that I was less literate than my counterparts, yet

I also realized that, perhaps especially in a situation where two are preparing for a shiur together, I was the ideal "student" or junior study partner. The situation is somewhat different from that of, say, a one-on-one competitive sport such as tennis or squash. There, as I noticed decades ago, the best partner is someone who's just a bit stronger than you are: you're in the game, but you always have to push yourself as hard as you can. That would mean that, for guys like Asher or Yisroel Ruven, I'm less than ideal if shared Talmud study is like a game of tennis. Yet, while social Talmud study can have competitive aspects, the fundamental logic of the interaction is not one of competition. Moreover, both Asher and Yisroel Ruven, in their time at the beis medresh, are learning but also learning to teach: so someone like me, who has good insights but less fluency than they do, is someone who can contribute to the group deliberations, but who can also be taught.

With Rabbi Karp

As my notes above reveal, Rabbi Karp himself also found time to study with me. I've known Rabbi Karp (or at least known who he was), since about the first time I came into the yeshiva in 1983 or 1984, but probably never had a conversation with him before December 2011. He is usually at the beis medresh during the day, also teaches at the Bialystoker Synagogue, and provides kashrut supervision for various businesses on the Lower East Side, though fewer and fewer as the neighborhood's kosher infrastructure shrinks. In addition, he is in charge of a small congregation on the Sabbath and holidays at the one remaining Jewish old age home in the neighborhood. His beard is snowy white.

Eventually, I decided that when Rabbi Karp had first asked if I was "looking for a chevrusa," perhaps he was offering to learn with me himself, though he didn't pose the question. So I said to him, "Of course, if you have time to study with me yourself, I would be honored."

"Thank you," he responded.

The next morning he added, "So you're here anyway, right? So I can find you. So I don't need your phone number," and I agreed. He asked me further, "Did you enjoy the [Rosh Yeshiva's] *Mishnah berurah* shiur?" This brought me back to my embarrassed moment on my first day in the yeshiva, when I had made the whole class stand while I introduced myself to the Rosh Yeshiva. Nevertheless, I told Rabbi Karp I had enjoyed that shiur, and so he invited me to join him and a partner for *Mishnah berurah* study after the Talmud shiur. Since Simcha was out, the 12:15 p.m. to 1:30 p.m. time slot was open for me. Rabbi Karp brought out an edition of *Mishnah berurah* I had never seen, with extensive footnotes summarizing arguments and halachic rulings of major twentieth-century halachic authorities. His study partner was Rabbi Weiss. When Rabbi Karp introduced us, Rabbi Weiss apologized to me: "I speak a little Yiddish—" meaning simply that some of his utterances are inevitably Yiddish. His English is fine, and he used it almost exclusively when I was with them, although I replied by assuring him in Yiddish that I would be happy to listen to his Yiddish as well.

The subject matter they were dealing with was the laws of heating water on Shabbes (*Mishnah berurah*, section 318). In detail. With many different opinions. Rabbi Karp and Rabbi Weiss referred to the footnotes documenting recent opinions (that is, those subsequent to the early twentieth-century *Mishnah berurah* itself) as "the numbers," since unlike the Hebrew letters used to indicate notes in the *Mishnah berurah*, these are indeed numbered. The sweetness of joining the discussion is inseparable from the details being considered, and yet I could not find a way to capture either the sweetness or the details adequately when I tried to "write up" this study experience just a few hours later. At the Rosh Yeshiva's shiur, it was possible at least to take discreet, sketchy notes. Here it seemed impossible.

Eventually I also had the chance to study one on one with Rabbi Karp. Although I was originally planning to spend just mornings in the yeshiva, Rabbi Karp told me that, if I could wait

for half an hour or so after minchah (thus, until around 2:30 p.m.),
he would have some time to study with me. He asked what I
wanted to study, and I said it didn't matter to me.

"Anything?" he double-checked.

"Anything," I confirmed, and so he chose to go over with me a
piece of Gemara in the tractate Bechoros, which covers the laws
governing the obligation to donate or redeem the firstborn of
cattle and humans to the Temple. This discussion at Bechoros folio
49 has to do with the proper timing for performance of redemption of the firstborn son from the *kohanim (priests)*, as dictated by
Scripture. Rather than our quite sharing the task, I would say that
he taught it to me—reading the text himself rather than asking me
to read (as Rabbi Goldman does); extracting from Rashi rather
than having both of us look at Rashi together. When we finished
I asked Rabbi Karp whether the Gemara we'd just reviewed was
the daf yomi, the "folio of the day" that is studied by thousands
worldwide in a coordinated schedule, since I knew that he had
been teaching daf yomi classes both at the Bialystoker Shul and at
the Fifth Avenue Synagogue uptown, a congregation with a very
different demographic mix. "Yes," he said; and so I had gotten my
personal daf yomi shiur that day.

My training as a lawyer, a profession I followed with mixed suc-
cess between receiving my PhD and becoming a full-time academic, helped me follow the argument in the Gemara. For example, I followed what was going on in a discussion of a
hypothetical situation: A father, the firstborn of his mother, had
never been redeemed from the kohanim and now has a son who
needs redemption. The father has enough liquid cash for one redemption. In addition, there is property that the father had previously sold, subject to a prior lien—that is, the property was collateral for a debt that the father has not yet repaid. Does the father's
obligation to redeem himself from the kohanim trump the prior
lien, meaning in effect that the obligation to redeem is itself a debt?
The Gemara rules that it does: the kohen can take the value of the

father's redemption from the sold property, and the father uses his own money to redeem the son.

Another day, Rabbi Karp asked me if I was interested in another chevrusa, from 3:30–4:30 p.m. I responded perhaps a bit too cautiously: "On some days," cautiously leaving myself the "out" of a shorter day should my patience flag. He, on the other hand, was remarkably content to leave the schedule open and ask me, from day to day, "Are you staying?"

I did stay until 4:30 p.m. most afternoons during my kollel year, and when the year ended I missed studying with Rabbi Karp. Home in New York from Ithaca for Thanksgiving break the following semester, I asked Rabbi Karp if I could join him and his young chevrusa for daf yomi study after lunch. "Are you doing it, or do you just want to drop in?" I wasn't sure what he meant by "doing it"; though I took him to be asking whether I was going to join them regularly, he might also have been asking whether I was keeping up with the daf yomi on my own.

"I'm doing it sometimes," I answered, thinking of the week this month I spent studying the beginning of tractate Yoma (about the laws of Yom Kippur) with an Israeli postdoc at Cornell.

His chevrusa was pleased to have me join them: "It's like last summer again."

Rabbi Karp said, "Okay, but it's gonna cost you. We're eating lunch, so you'll have to 'say' it." Really, I think he was just giving me a chance to practice parsing the text aloud. So I would say a few words, and he would either correct me or not, while he explained and commented at length. At the end (and long before we'd learned the whole folio, though the discipline of daf yomi is to cover a folio every day) he said, "Well, unfortunately I have to stop now. You did excellent—you can come back tomorrow."

I learned something about my mother from Rabbi Karp one day when, not for the first time, but a little more explicitly with me now that he knew me better, he expressed his sense of being overwhelmed, asking in Yiddish: "Vu halt men in der velt?" (What's our place or situation in the world?)

Indeed, my mother in her late years would sometimes complain to me on the telephone, "I don't know where I am in the world." I always thought of it as psychobabble rather than Yiddishism.

This time I responded, also in Yiddish, "bay *der* mishne," at *this* mishnah. That would have been good enough, but I added somewhat self-righteously, "that's the only sure place we have."

He responded, "gut gezogt," well said.

Somehow, Rabbi Karp's identification with the place seems to afford him a fine awareness of the tensions between rabbinic grandeur and Lower East Side matter-of-factness that help make MTJ special. Four examples:

- One day Rabbi Karp found a broken watch in the lunchroom—a watch face and part of a band. He held it up, asking, "Anybody lose half a watch? Anybody lose half a watch?" He knew it was funny and he also knew that the humor in it has something to do with the nature of the place, that old East Side with its lack of pretense and its ability to make do with not quite enough.

- Another day he held up a piece of paper that he'd found in an old volume in the yeshiva, and excitedly brought it to show to an elderly gentleman who spends a fair amount of time learning by himself at the table at the back of the room. I was curious as well, and Rabbi Karp explained to the two of us that this is a holy relic of the old Mashgiach, Rabbi Michel Barenbaum. "See if you can make out the message" (in the tone of someone who has discovered an ancient text full of meaning for us today). We did. It said in Hebrew, "If you take this out from the library, please return it when you're done."

- On December 25, 2012, knowing that Elissa was not well, I was itching to get home and approached Rabbi Karp to see if he could start with me a bit earlier than usual. "Okay, I have to go into the siyum [in the Rosh Yeshiva's 2:00 p.m. shiur], but let's do a few minutes." He opened to the very bottom of Shabbes 83a: "Oh, it's appropriate [to this situation, when we just have a few minutes to learn together]: 'One should not refrain from going to the beis medresh [even] for [only] an hour. . . . For [in that very hour] we had explained to us a mishnah we'd been struggling with for years.'" The explanation of the mishnah in question had to do with the requirements for an object to be susceptible to ritual impurity. Rabbi Karp summarized: "It has to be portable . . . and it has to have the characteristics of a sack. So that's another thing that's appropriate for today" (a clear allusion to Santa Claus).

Even though I still spend time in the yeshiva, I sometimes grow nostalgic for my kollel year. On the afternoon before the holiday of Shemini Atzeres, during October 2014, Rabbi Karp wished me "a gut kvitl," may your "receipt" for the coming year be a good one. Offering such a wish, which comes after one's fate is presumably "sealed" on Yom Kippur, is a hasidic custom that has spread, like many others, to the broader Orthodox population.

I said, "I miss learning with you."

He: "Me too."

I: "I want to do it again."

He: "Alright, next [time you have a] sabbatical."

With Nasanel

My friend Nasanel first captured my attention with his rather loud monologues about pedagogy in the middle of the beis medresh. Eventually I said something to him about his ideas, even though we hadn't been introduced. He said, "Oh, you heard that," making me feel as though I'd been eavesdropping, though it was probably hard for anybody in the room at the time not to hear what he'd been saying. But this young man I was meeting for the first time clearly wasn't offended, and wanted to know more about me. He asked me where I had "learned," that is, attended yeshiva; it seems

I gave him the impression of knowing more than I thought I did. When he found out what I do for a living, he started coming with questions about English usage, showing me (for example) an ArtScroll commentary that refers to "Job's paean to the Almighty," and asking me what "paean" means.

Over the course of my kollel year and beyond, he became a good friend, and my respect for his intelligence and integrity continued to grow. After a few months he became one of my regular study partners. At his suggestion, we began by studying the Mishnah of Kilaim, which deals with forbidden and permitted combinations of various species planted in the same field. As usual, he did most of the talking, though I gradually introduced some balance in the pace of our study. Nasanel both frustrated and fascinated me with an elaborate account likening the various rabbis' views as to the amount of admixture required before a sown field is impermissible to the military strategies of Clausewitz and Sun Tzu for conquering and dividing enemies and territories. It came in a torrent of words that I could never come close to capturing in a notepad, nor on a tape recorder, and perhaps not even with a video camera: perhaps these words are not meant to be captured.

When we started studying Mishnah together, I had mentioned that I like to study Symcha Petrushka's translation and commentary in Yiddish. Nasanel was delighted, because he recalls his grandfather spending time with that text. When we first discussed it, Nasanel mentioned he'd heard "from a relative" that Petrushka had been a *maskil*, a Jewish Enlightener, and thus religiously suspect.

A passerby, hearing this, was incensed: "Where did you hear that? Petrushka was frum!" Nasanel backed down, but he did notice a point in Petrushka where the author cited a text by a *gelernter*, that is, a [secular] scholar—and took to calling Petrushka "der Gelernter."

Rabbi Schuster—a member of the Kloyzenburger hasidic community—had pleased me very much the week before by inquiring about Petrushka's Yiddish Mishnah. I was able to bring in the volume he wanted and lend it to him, and eventually I presented him with a full set, which I had ordered from the Yiddish Book Center. Nasanel photographed the presentation on his cell phone: "I want to record this! Worlds meet! The New School presents a gift to Kloyzenburg!"

Indeed, Nasanel was so taken with studying this edition of the Mishnah that in addition to having me read Petrushka's discussion of every mishnah as part of our process of studying the tractate Kilaim, he decided he also wanted me to read to him Petrushka on the Mishnah in Berachos, which deals substantially with the daily recitation of the Shema prayer (beginning "Hear O Israel, the Lord our God, the Lord is One"). Nasanel explained to me that he knows Berachos quite well.

> At some point, when I was less mature than now, I was learning Berachos very intensely. There's a sefer by Rabbi Perlow, a commentary on Rav Saadya Gaon's *Sefer mitzvos* that goes through every view of every *rishon* [medieval commentator] in great detail. Rabbi Perlow makes it clear that 90 percent of the rishonim hold that we are only biblically obligated to recite in our daily prayers the first verse of the Shema, 10 percent say the first paragraph is a biblical obligation, and there's maybe one view with a real *yeshivishe kvetsh* [abstruse reasoning] who holds that all three paragraphs are biblically mandated. Wow, I just explained that to you in thirty seconds, and Rabbi Perlow could have done so, too. Anyway, I spent a vast amount of time on the first folio of Berachos, so I know it pretty well. My chevrusa—

> I interrupted: "You put a chevrusa through this?"

> "I did. Eventually he got a job. He was too much of a gentleman [to say, 'I've had it and I'm not learning this with you anymore'], so he got a job instead."

After completing Kilaim, Nasanel and I turned from Mishnah study to begin the section of the *Tur* that deals with marriage and family law. One day he walked with me during our usual pre-minchah study period downtown to J&R Music World, where I had to return a piece of stereo equipment. I showed him the Catholic church among the courthouses at Foley Square, which bears the motto, "Beati qui ambulant in lege Domini"—blessed are those who walk in God's law. He thought it unbearably smug and self-serving, and then said, "Ah, but you're a lawyer [so you'd like it]." We stopped on the way back by the cemetery of the Spanish and Portuguese Synagogue at Chatham Square, where Nasanel composed a prayer, in English, out loud, to the souls buried there to help him with his learning, while he's still in this world, and he offered them in exchange more than their share of the merit that would be accumulated in the course of that study.

Like my other study partners, Nasanel is also remarkably understanding of my inconstancy: as the Rosh Yeshiva said to me once when, in an uncharacteristically formal move, I took my leave of him following a winter break: "You have to work." Still, it can be hard to find the time, and to pick up right where we left off. One day I had agreed with Nasanel that we were going to study the *Tur* after shiur. But the shiur ended early, and I didn't see him, so I went and rejoined Asher and Hillel for intense review of the Rashis and Tosafos that we'd looked at before and during the shiur—and finally began to get a bit of a sense of what was going on. I thought Nasanel hadn't come in at all, but then I saw him at minchah and he explained he'd seen me learning with Asher and Hillel and didn't want to interrupt me.

When Nasanel and I eventually did sit down to learn together, around 3:00 p.m., I was once again amazed at the torrent of words and references that come out of his mouth—that day, largely focused on historical precedents for rejecting the intrusive spying on private correspondence that was very much in the news just then. He spoke about Henry Stimson, as secretary of war, finding out that the United States was intercepting telegraph communications from the enemy and putting a stop to it, saying, "Gentlemen don't read each other's correspondence."

Then we sat down to finish the introduction to the *Beis Yosef*, since Nasanel quite commendably believes in reading introductions and other explanatory notes. In the last paragraphs, Joseph Karo explains his strategy of looking at the views of the three great rishonim known as the Rosh, the Rif, and the Rambam, and deciding according to the majority of those three. Nasanel professed to be incensed at this: he believes it's an unsubtle and unsophisticated legal strategy, unauthorized by rabbinic tradition, and that the subsequent freezing of halacha in the *Shulchan aruch* has largely caused the disastrous falling away from Torah Judaism in recent centuries. I replied that this was interesting to consider, but I had always thought that what happened is that in the modern period, the pace of social change was just too rapid for the processes of halachic adjustment to keep up with.

During my Thanksgiving break in 2013, Nasanel and I resumed our slowly progressing study of the *Tur*. We decided to learn while standing. I used the one real *shtender* (lectern) in the beis medresh, while Nasanel, somewhat taller than I, rested his copy on the top of the bookcase that holds the prayer books. Nasanel's copy is part of a set that I recently purchased for him as a gift, inspired by his complaint that he'd like to be looking at the same (new) edition that I have. It seemed that standing together inside the beis medresh worked better than either sitting across each other at a table in the beis medresh (where I often felt that Nasanel's loud voice was distracting others, and that I, as his study partner, was complicit), or the awkward alternative of learning out in the hallway while Nasanel waited to see the Rosh Yeshiva.

Another day, Nasanel and I decided to go into the library to study *Tur* together. Rabbi Fiedler and his chevrusa, and another study pair—that is, four men in all—were there already, continuing what they had been studying before the Mashgiach began his mussar shmues in the beis medresh. Nasanel and I sat close to each other in the back, started reading the first few words of a new chapter together, and I reminded him: "Speak softly and to the point," earning Rabbi Fiedler's clear approval. Nasanel began lecturing about the medical implications of the biblical category of *petsua daka*, roughly, a male with crushed testicles. Someone in this category is under the ban stated by Scripture as *lo yavo bekahal* (he shall not enter the collective), which the rabbis interpret as a ban against such a person marrying a Jewish woman of good lineage. Nasanel explained his understanding that this ban was based on inability to procreate, then considered exceptions based on medical science and in vitro fertilization. Eventually Rabbi Fiedler lost patience: "Nasanel, this is a library in a yeshiva, not a library in a university. You're lecturing now."

Nasanel: "It's all Torah."

Fiedler: "No, if it was Torah it wouldn't distract me. You're lecturing on talmudic science." What's pleasantly ironic about this is that Rabbi Fiedler clearly appreciates that I'm trying to keep Nasanel focused on learning and on the text (and reasonably quiet), rather than seeing me as a subversive or "foreign" influence on Nasanel.

Nasanel himself has not always been quite sure how far he should trust me. Once he confided in me an account of an awkward question that had been posed to the Rosh Yeshiva.

I asked Nasanel when he had heard this from the Rosh Yeshiva. "In shiur . . . he'll tell things like that, depending on who's around, if it's all insiders he can trust." Then Nasanel added: "There's somebody who doesn't entirely trust you in the shiur, who would like to take your notebook away."

I said, "Yisroel Ruven?"

But then Nasanel made clear that it was one side of himself, looking at my own ambivalence: "You [Jonathan] want to be part of the club" (but you want to be part of that "other" club, too, the one in the university).

I said, "I may never publish any of this."

"Yeah, but you tell your students about it."

In fact, my impression is that the Rosh Yeshiva has never watched his words in shiur when I'm there, neither before nor after I asked his permission to publish this book. I think rather this was an opportunity for Nasanel to record once again some of his own ambivalence, and to remind me that there is some potential risk to everyone in my participation.

At first, our routine in studying this text (set by Nasanel) was to read through one entire chapter of the *Tur*, then the *Beis Yosef* and then the commentary of the *Bach*—all dealing with the same topics. This may leave something to be desired in terms of comprehension, since a chapter of the *Tur* covers many detailed and often disputed points within a given topic. This procedure is, however, an efficient way of covering the entire page. It meant that when we started reading the commentary of the *Bach* on chapter 5, we were having the third round of our discussion / argument / one-way harangue about the reasons why Israelite males who are genitally maimed may not marry into the congregation. The *Bach* discusses the issue of whether a kohen who is *petsua daka* may marry a female convert (whom a "kosher" kohen would not be able to marry according to biblical law).

The case is discussed in the Gemara by analogy, drawn by Rav Sheisis, to his own ruling that an Israelite who is *petsua daka* may marry a female Gibeonite. The name Gibeonite appears in the book of Joshua as that of a group who are understood as having been problematically integrated in the course of the Israelite conquest. In the Gemara, Rav Sheisis's view is countered by Rava, who nevertheless later retracted. Thus, there is basis for later authorities to rule either way, and the ruling, as I understand it, relates to a dispute over whether the Gibeonites had been "bad" Jews (hence subject to the rules of bastardy pertinent to Jews, and suspect of bastard lineages because they had not been fully observant) or never Jewish at all (hence not subject to rules of bastardy that apply only to Jews). Most authorities rule like Rav Sheisis that this kohen may marry a female Gibeonite, thus holding that they never had been Jewish. However, the twelfth-century Baal Hamaor, who Nasanel tells me was famous for ignoring other rishonim and ruling his own way, follows the ruling of Rava before he retracted, thus implicitly holding that the Gibeonites had been properly Jewish.

Nasanel, who dreams of making me into an unambiguously believing, knowledgeable, and Torah-true halachic decisor, then asked how I rule on this case. I said that I thought the kohen should be allowed to marry this Gibeonite female. This amused Nasanel very much, since as he understood (but I didn't quite understand until he explained it to me) I had evidently allowed my desire to rule leniently to lead me into the "racist" view that the Gibeonites had never really been Jewish at all.

A different afternoon around 4:00 p.m., Nasanel came over and sat next to me and Asher. Though he had an open ArtScroll Gemara on the desk, I couldn't help thinking that he was sitting near us because he didn't have anybody to learn with and he was waiting for me to start resuming our joint study of the *Tur*. I found this distracting, and I also felt a bit guilty, so I said to him, "Nasanel, let's learn at five." While sitting with me and Asher, Nasanel recalled a story he'd told me in the morning. The original occasion for the story had been a discussion in shiur about a putative reference in the Gemara to a certain species of goose with external genitalia. I had remarked to him privately afterward that I didn't believe there had ever been any birds, geese or otherwise, with external genitalia. "Rabbi——at Slobodke once was learning with a baal teshuva there, and the guy pointed out that the Gemara was inconsistent with a map. So Rabbi——refused to learn with him anymore. But Reb Yaakov Kamenetsky came up with a *teruts* [resolution] to make the map consistent with the Gemara. And the Rosh Yeshiva says that there's no problem bringing a map in to try to understand the Gemara." At issue here, of course, was the extent to which "secular" knowledge about the world should be deemed pertinent to our engagement with and reception of the discourse in and around the Gemara.

While telling this, Nasanel said something about *baalei teshuva* (penitents). He added "meaning no disrespect," thus suggesting that I would assume he was thinking of me as someone who fit this category of "returnees" to the practice of halachic Judaism.

I fired back without thinking much, "I'm not a baal teshuva."

Nasanel then, and later when the two of us were sitting together, remonstrated that baal teshuva is a badge of honor; as the Gemara says (Berachos 34b), "In the place where the baal teshuva stands, even the most righteous among us cannot stand." Doubtless my knee-jerk response made it sound like I didn't want to be tarred with that label. Later I finally said to him, very quietly, "I'm not a baal teshuva because I don't have *kharote* [remorse]." So Nasanel said, "Yes, the Rambam does require remorse if you're going to be a baal teshuva."

Nasanel's goals of making me a scholar and making me a Torah Jew appear sometimes in tandem, sometimes in tension with each other. One Sunday morning neither Hillel, Asher, nor Yisroel Ruven was available to me. And since the shiur is only held from Monday through Thursday, we didn't have a shiur to prepare for that day, either. Nasanel and I took the opportunity to study together from around 10:40 a.m. until noon, an unusually long stretch for us. And we actually got through a good deal of the *Beis Yosef*. He goes a bit faster than I can follow, though I chalk it up to reading practice. Still, he consistently finds points in the text we're studying to hammer home the larger lessons he seemingly wants sometimes just to articulate to himself, and sometimes to convey to me. Often he pushes me to ask "why"—Why is the halacha this way or that? What is the larger theological or philosophical point?— rather than just continuing to play it safe with the "what," a more neutral stance that doesn't require me to decide between my academic and yeshivish views.

At one point he returned to the theme of sibling rivalry. Nasanel knew that my older brother Daniel is a leading academic Talmudist, and had earlier made much of my presumed envy of my brother's learning and reputation, mostly because he wants me to think less like my brother and more like himself—although he might say he wants me to think more for my own self. He framed the question of sibling rivalry or influence in terms of the masters these two disciples might follow: my brother, he knew, studied with Professor Saul Lieberman, a product of the Lithuanian yeshiva system whose works were effectively banned in the yeshiva world because he taught at the Conservative Jewish Theological Seminary. By contrast, Nasanel fervently wants me to be more fully devoted to our Rosh Yeshiva.

I told Nasanel: "I'm here!" (What more do you want from me?)

"Yes, part of you is here, but I want to convert the rest of you."

There it was, that word "convert," precisely what I've been telling people outside the yeshiva world that the people inside the beis medresh weren't trying to do to me. If Nasanel wants me to become more "faithful," he's discreet enough that he rarely speaks of that desire. In any case, I can stand the occasional hint that he's not quite satisfied with me as I am, precisely because in the midst of his zeal Nasanel sees me so clearly. He calls my Ithaca-professor side "childish," and, in a voice mail a day or two earlier, had told me that he "doesn't like academics, but that's okay because there's another side to you that I do like very much." I, of course, resist being divided up in this way. In fact, Nasanel's challenges help me understand and refine the question that does interest me very much, professionally and personally, of whether it's really possible to specify a place where religious "belief" stops and secular "skepticism" begins.

Still, that day Nasanel's pushing me to fit in better did bother me somewhat. I started to feel a pressure I don't want, and freedom from that pressure is one of the themes of this book. The story would be neater if MTJ always provided me the range of freedom that I often do enjoy there.

Perhaps in self-defense, I reminded Nasanel that he was my "informant": "One of these days I'm just going to tape you for an hour and a half." Actually, Nasanel's unrelenting and brilliant attacks on my secular side leave me with the conviction that, if I could get him on videotape (or even record without video), I could distill his discourse into productive meditations for academics about the religious/secular divide. I even thought of explaining to him that that was why I'd like to videotape him—a prospect I'd already tentatively raised, and of which he was naturally suspicious.

"Okay, but only you and your son can listen to it." (I guess he'd like to be an influence on Jonah as well.)

"Fine, but the notes [the ones I write down myself] are all mine!" I retorted.

During the school year, I'm usually only in the yeshiva every few weeks, and then only briefly. My summertime attendance is sporadic as well, so that my steadiest attendance is during those times when I'm not teaching upstate yet the Rosh Yeshiva is still holding his Gemara shiur. Those times are from mid-May through the end of June, and my winter break in December and January. After shiur on May 14, 2014, Nasanel and I discussed resuming our study of the beginning of the *Tur*. I suggested that we might perhaps skip the *Beis Yosef*, which I had already been through once on my own, and go straight to the commentary of the *Bach*. Nasanel responded, "No, we might as well do the whole thing. I'm going to be learning with you for eternity anyway, so there's no need for shortcuts."

By a year later, perhaps because he was getting a bit impatient in this world, Nasanel decided that we might, at least for now, better concentrate on getting through just the text of the *Tur* itself. "If I was confident that once you retire, you're going to be learning full time, we might go slower. But you probably want to go traveling around the South of France and tasting wine in the Finger Lakes."

Nasanel expressed frustration that I had been absent for so long, and admitted it was hard to fall back into the rhythm of learning with me again. He suggested I sell our apartment, move to Brooklyn, live on the difference, and learn full time. "And you don't have to go off to Frankfurt" (and other distant places to give papers and prove that I'm a credible secular academic).

Perhaps part of the reason he was out of sorts with me for being away for so long was that interrupted conversations had been on his mind all along. Given my ear for a few minutes, he brought up again the issue of the commandment to Moses to eradicate the Amalekites. He recognizes this as an episode of genocide, but he ultimately accepts it on the grounds of "we're right and they're wrong."

I told him this argument carried no weight with me, then wondered aloud why he was even talking about it, until he reminded me that months ago I told him I wouldn't obey that commandment to Moses. (The Rosh Yeshiva told him the commandment is not in force today; other rabbis have told him it is.) He argued, "You wouldn't do it for the same reason you don't want to go outside in bad weather [to study something with him that is not appropriate to learn in the beis medresh]. It's because you're too tied to *olam hazeh* [this world and its things]."

For some time Nasanel, who usually arrives from Brooklyn shortly after 11:00 a.m., just in time for the Rosh Yeshiva's shiur, began coming early in the morning. And so, one morning, at his suggestion, I arrived at the yeshiva to learn with him at 9:15 a.m., but he had too much talking to do. Eventually I closed the *Tur*, and he said, "No, don't, we're going to get to it soon." I tell him I was worried the book might catch a cold, and he was pleased: "Oh, you believe books have *neshomos* [souls]?" This led me to admit, somewhat reluctantly, my abandonment decades ago of a beautiful, large two-volume set of Maimonides's *Mishneh Torah* printed in Germany in the nineteenth century (we were moving to a new apartment, albeit in the same building, and somehow I just couldn't bring it along upstairs), prefacing my admission as the worst thing I've ever done. He was properly horrified, but insisted that I must not have understood what I was doing. (In fact, I knew what the book was, though I don't think I could have made head nor tail of it then.) As a kind of penitence, he gave me a set of a two-volume commentary by a certain nineteenth-century rabbi, recently reprinted. There was a box of them in the yeshiva, and Nasanel had agreed to get them distributed. . . . I left it at the beis medresh, confident that it would still be there the next day.

Another day as we sat over the *Tur*, Nasanel's daily harangue was on the topic of voluntary and compulsory divorce in Jewish law. The problem is that divorce can only be granted by the husband, and it must be granted willingly. When a husband is recalcitrant, therefore, the Gemara indicates that stronger measures are called for (although the Rosh Yeshiva stated, during our study of the tractate Gittin, that in our current diasporic conditions we are not empowered to deploy violence). "We beat him up," Nasanel paraphrased the Gemara, "until he says he wants to give her a divorce. It's like the Inquisition."

Here I interjected, "lehavdil," a phrase I learned when I first began studying Yiddish. "Lehavdil," a Hebrew infinitive, means "to distinguish," and is interjected whenever someone risks making inappropriate comparisons between the sacred and the profane.

Nasanel accordingly added, "lehavdil," and went on, "but we're right and they're wrong. The Inquisition was saying, 'in your heart of hearts you really want to repent, and we're just helping you to resist the Devil and do what you really want to do.'"

What caught my attention here was the "but we're right and they're wrong," which Nasanel seemed to utter almost as a gloss on "lehavdil." The intertext, alluded to earlier, is the several times over the past few years that he has confronted the legacy of genocidal injunctions from the Torah (about utterly wiping out every trace of Amalek). Nasanel had reiterated and elaborated on the idea that ultimately it may not be possible or pertinent to justify this command in terms of universal morality, but rather, "we're right and they're wrong" (the Torah tells us to do this). I had already told him I wouldn't be able to carry out such a command. Here, of course, it was he who brought up the analogy of "forced voluntarism" in Jewish law to "forced voluntary confession" by the Inquisition, and then uttered his own "we're right and they're wrong," thus cordoning off observations about Jewish law and practice from the necessary critique of Gentile ways.

On another occasion, Nasanel was trying to articulate the logic behind the category of the *zonah*. The term is generally translated as "prostitute," but clearly includes a broader range of "fallen women," to borrow the Victorian term. I suggested an analysis in terms of the pure and the impure, à la Mary Douglas, but Nasanel responded, "No, there you go with your spiritual stuff again, you have to think about it rationally." I certainly didn't think I was giving a spiritual argument, but in his eyes, he was the rationalist here.

This association of piety with rationalism, famously (indeed, stereotypically) characteristic of the Lithuanian yeshivas and of Litvak Jewishness more generally, is also closely linked to the interrogation of personal motives associated with the Mussar movement. Once I was speaking with Nasanel about my on-and-off plans to pay for a memorial plaque for my grandfather on the wall of the beis medresh. Nasanel discouraged me: "Memorialization doesn't really mean having your name written down somewhere. It's the good deeds you do that memorialize your ancestors. If you try to honor him with a plaque, he's really paying part of it [presumably because of the recognition he's getting in this world, when after his death he should be entitled to his full reward in the World to Come]. Your *zeydie* [grandfather] will be happier to see you [when I join him there] if you just do the mitzvos instead."

Then he told me the following story: When his grandfather died, his father hadn't wanted to sleep in the bed where his own father had slept. One night his father's father came to his father in a dream, and said, "Alter, get up from the floor."

His father said, "Dad, it's so wonderful to see you." Then the grandfather turned around and started to walk out the door of the room.

"Dad, where are you going?"

"To *beis din* [a rabbinical court] with Naftoli." Naftoli was a close relative, and there had been a long-standing feud.

"And it was [really like] they were going to the *beis din shel maale* [heavenly court], because within the span of a few years all the people in the family who were part of that feud, who were of varying ages, died."

By now you know Nasanel fairly well, so let me just share a few more quick snapshots that may add to your impression of him:

- 10/15/14: Nasanel is on a monologue for half an hour on various topics, one stringing from the previous. I ask him, "Could you do this all day?" He replies without missing a beat, "Yes," and continues.
- 12/18/13: Text messages from Nasanel the past few days:
  - "Please bring Thucydides's *Peloponnesian War*." He had been reading Herodotus, and his main reaction—at least as he expressed it to me—was how awful the people Herodotus describes were, and how badly the Greek gods come off in Herodotus's account: worse, he says, than in Homer. I told him he should read Thucydides, who's much more "scientific" than Herodotus.
  - "I feel relieved when on any given subject through logical discussion catharsis has been achieved." To which I replied: "Yes I know but I do not always endorse the premises on which your dilemmas are based." "Yes of course," he replied.
- 3/3/15: Nasanel (walking with me to the butcher store, and then all the way home, holding his prayer book and the tzedakah collection can because he followed me out just before the end of minchah): "Learning with you is my top priority. Saving your soul is secondary."

A Chevrusa Can Be More than Two

You've already been introduced to Asher Stoler and Yisroel Ruven Hersh, but it took me a few days to learn their names, even when I had been introduced to them and started joining them to prepare for the Gemara shiur. I quickly noticed that they are the two most active interlocutors in the shiur—the only ones, in fact, who will unfailingly catch the Rosh Yeshiva's attention when they respond or interrupt him with a question or suggestion. The first few days

I joined them to prepare for an hour before the shiur, there were a couple of basic points that I missed as we were going through the text. Somehow, everything I didn't understand was explained to me whether I asked about it or not. And not much that I did understand was laid out for me: I was somewhat astounded at the ability of the various people I'm studying with to gauge what I do and don't know. Perhaps I was good at communicating it as well.

Nor was I interrogated before I could join the group. A few weeks after I started, I walked in to find Asher at his usual morning place. Yisroel Ruven was in the beis medresh, but hadn't sat down yet. Asher prompted me: "So you live in North Carolina?" I explained that Elissa and I were only there during the semester, but when I don't have to be in school we're here in New York, and that I liked North Carolina very much, although Jewishly it was thin for me. I also explained that when I was there, I wasn't quite as strict about Jewish observance. Rather than offering either a judgmental or even a mollifying direct response, he merely said, "Yeah, it's nice down there, but it's a lot slower, right? I used to go to Myrtle Beach [in South Carolina]. So I'd go see the Chabad rabbi there, a very nice fellow. I told him I commute on the F train, and he said, 'Oh, New York is so noisy, I can't take it there!'"

I was certainly the beginner in the group, but recognized that there were some things I contribute to the collective understanding. Asher seemed to appreciate that I recognized one of Rashi's terms, spelled something like *tserises*, and which, in context, clearly referred to cherries. I helped myself by reviewing the pertinent section of the Gemara with ArtScroll's elucidation before coming to yeshiva. Yet, when Asher and I sat down together one morning when it was just the two of us, he found questions that ArtScroll had not answered, or had glossed over or had not seen—such that I began to appreciate more fully that the very opening up of questions is a key to being a real participant in these discourses.

On the one hand, I, and before me Hillel, had been invited to join Asher and Yisroel Ruven, and were clearly more than welcome. On the other hand, the two of them clearly constituted a longtime chevrusa. One morning in late December 2011, the segment they were preparing for that day's shiur concerned the effect of deafness and muteness on the capacity to perform the ceremony of *yibum* (marrying the widow of a dead brother who has died childless, known in English as levirate marriage) and *chalitzah* (renunciation of yibum). The short answer is that a deaf-mute can perform yibum, for which only a physical act is required, but not chalitzah, whose ceremonial form is biblically prescribed and requires actual speech. The Gemara presents various permutations of deaf-mute and hearing pairs of brothers and sisters married to each other, and the legal consequences of various eventualities. Yisroel Ruven didn't understand the point of a comment by Rashi. "What's Rashi telling us here, Asher? Asher, please, help me out."

Asher was silent for a few minutes, looking at other commentators, and then responded, "Rashash says Rashi is telling us that the fact that one of the sisters or brothers is not disabled doesn't make a difference."

Another morning we were preparing a passage in Gittin that dealt with the validity or invalidity of a man's declaration to his wife that she is hereby divorced, subject to various stipulations. With Yisroel Ruven reading and glossing the text for the group, and Hillel and me actively participating in the discussion, Asher sat quite silent. Eventually we stopped to mark that he seemed unhappy. He was bothered by a move made early on in the passage, although I didn't quite understand his objection. But he did try to state it clearly, and when Yisroel Ruven resisted engaging with it, said, "Yisroel Ruven, don't dance with me!" Later on, somewhat mollified, he joked, "Ok, I'll dance with you later."

As we got up to go into the shiur, Yisroel Ruven said, "Asher, I'm worried that I'm losing you."

Asher replied, "Sometimes it's rocky but we'll always be together."

Asher made the analogy between a chevrusa and a marriage explicit one day, as we were walking along East Broadway to hear a shmues by a very elderly and revered rabbi, one of the last surviving members of the Mir Yeshiva group who had spent World War II as refugees in Shanghai. Asher remarked that today, finding a chevrusa is like finding a marriage partner. "But a relative of mine told me that in Europe, you'd be sitting there, and someone would walk in, and you'd say, 'Do you want to learn?' and you'd learn together for a year, and then that would be it, and you'd never really know much about the guy. It's definitely *yeridas hadoros* [a decline in the quality of our generation]." Asher was observing that today, we're more finicky about who we partner with—and perhaps implying as well that the emphasis is more on ourselves and each other, and less on the Torah that we're learning in and for itself.

Learning the tractate Bava Kama one day with just Asher and Hillel, I found myself more than once amazed and puzzled at the amount of time and energy they were willing to spend attempting a hermeneutic rescue of what seemed on its face a very unlikely hypothetical in the Gemara. The general issue was the relation between a party's control of space and his potential liability for damage caused by his possessions. At one point, the Gemara entertains and ultimately rejects the notion that the mouth of one's animal might be considered part of that person's "domain," and therefore the damage that is caused by one's animal within its mouth—that is, by its act of eating—entails no liability on the owner's part. Usually I go along with these extended considerations of strained hypotheticals, but this time I couldn't help thinking to myself, "Why are you guys worrying so much about something the Gemara has already told us it rejects?" The answer, I'm sure, would be: if the Gemara thought it was worthwhile raising the possibility, then there must be a certain plausibility to it, even if it's hard to see.

Looking for those plausible scenarios can be an occasion for humor; at the yeshiva, devotion to Torah is not always equated with "seriousness." Hillel, Asher, and I prepared together the Gemara on Bava Kama 34b. The text there presents a hypothetical, where, after an ox has been gored and killed, its carcass rises in value (from the standpoint of a prospective Gentile buyer) from the time of its death until the time of its sale. This seemed unlikely, as even if the market is moving quickly, the carcass is rotting faster. We speculated about what circumstances could lead to such a rise in value.

I said, "Hey, it's aged beef!"

Asher: "Yeah, make sure it's got lots of flies on it.'"

Hillel: "Make sure the hide shrank." This last echoed one of the classic reasons for presuming that the carcass loses value from the time of death to the time of sale. Such moments where we toss out implausible hypotheticals provide the chevrusa not only with a chance to bond through joking, but to engage in some intercultural play. At this moment we were imagining what it is that might possibly attract (or to be more precise, imagining what the rabbis might have imagined attracting) Gentile buyers to a rotting animal's corpse. This was also an occasion for rhetorical separation of Jews from Gentiles. Rather than being dependent on any claims made about "actual" Gentile culture or values, we were, instead, semiknowingly (and with some uneasy conscience, at least on my part) creating our own "virtual" Gentiles.

This study group revolved around Asher, or around Asher and Yisroel Ruven, and occasionally others would join us for a day or a week, shifting the detailed patterns of study in unpredictable ways. One day, someone whom I recognized but who was not in the yeshiva regularly was sitting with Asher and Hillel when I came in around 10:15 a.m. He was using an ArtScroll Talmud, although (unlike me when I'm studying on my own) mostly not looking at the English. They were struggling over the very last column in the third chapter of Bava Kama, trying to get a sense of the meaning of the Gemara's first explanation of the Mishnah, which reads, "If two oxen belonging to one man were chasing another man's ox and the other man's ox was gored, both of them are liable." We struggled, until the man using the ArtScroll offered to tell us how that edition explained this text.

Asher resisted: "No, let's try to figure it out ourselves for a while first."

I said: "He [Asher] doesn't let me do it [bring in the ArtScroll explanation]."

The visitor said: "Yeah, but I don't do it all the time." (Did he think I "do it all the time?")

A few minutes later Asher asked, "Does ArtScroll have anything to say about that?"

What ArtScroll explained is that what appears to be a definitive ruling is actually to be read as an incredulous question. That way, everything becomes clear.

For Asher and Yisroel Ruven, the purpose of preparing for the shiur is precisely that: being ready to be good students of the Rosh Yeshiva, in the double sense of receptivity to his distinctive analysis of the texts, and being good interlocutors who can help make the shiur a seminar and not just a lecture. Part of being good interlocutors is knowing as thoroughly as possible where and when, through the centuries of written commentary, one's own questions have already been asked and often answered. One day late in the winter of 2014, a difficult Tosafos kept us in shiur until 12:30 p.m. While Asher, Hillel, and I were preparing beforehand, Asher had come up with an explanation of it. He proposed it to the Rosh Yeshiva in shiur, but the Rosh Yeshiva wasn't convinced by Asher's explanation (or we might have gotten out earlier). The next day the Rosh Yeshiva said to Asher that he had checked, and the proposal Asher gave was the same as that of the Maharsha.

Asher's reaction to that was silence. Either way, he said, you lose; either you admit that you didn't bother to check the Maharsha, or you did, and you're not giving credit where credit is due. This reminded Asher of an anecdote from his own adolescent yeshiva years. One of the boys had proposed an answer to a problem in the Gemara that turned out to have been given in the thirteenth century by the scholar known as Rashba. The teacher responded angrily: "I'm going to smack you in the face!" (for having the chutzpah to propose the Rashba's answer without attribution even if the kid had never seen it there).

Sometimes, then, it's risky not to turn the pages of the volume, to check thoroughly with the authorities whose commentaries are reprinted at the back. And occasionally, doing so produces an unexpected reward. This happened when we began the study of Bava Kama in the Rosh Yeshiva's shiur. Asher brought in a volume from a set that was smaller than the editions of the tractates Gittin and Sotah that he had used. He told me that it had belonged to his uncle. One day Asher showed me a piece of paper he'd found stuck between the pages of that volume, and asked me what it was about, since the text was in Yiddish. It was the title page of a book of *segules* and *refues*—the first half a translation into Yiddish of a text containing a variety of folk formulas for healing various medical problems; the second, a collection of medicines, available either over the counter or by prescription, again for a range of ailments. I was intrigued by the combination of "mystical" and practical approaches, and would have liked to have at least a photocopy of this sheet. Asher closed the Gemara on the sheet, and a few weeks later reported to me that he had not been able to find it again. "It disappeared! It's absolutely not there anymore! It's something you should write in your book."

He mentioned it again when I came in, around 10:00 a.m., on the first day of an extended weekend in New York City that I'd carved out of my first semester at Cornell in the fall of 2013. He had just finished telling Hillel about his grandfather, who had moved to Israel at an advanced age and quite ill, when no one expected him to live more than a year. His grandfather had taken in the view from his new home in Jerusalem, and said, "I could live for another ten years." And he did. Exactly. And that reminded Asher of the story about the page in his grandfather's Gemara . . . which reminded me of a story by S. An-sky, "In Khorostkov during the First World War," that Jack Kugelmass and I included in our book *From a Ruined Garden*. There An-sky reported that when the front lines came close to the town and the Jews had to evacuate, a hasidic antiquarian and bookdealer secreted some precious manuscripts in a wall, including a letter in the hand of the Baal Shem-Tov. When the Jews returned after the fighting stopped and retrieved the manuscripts, the letter was found, but all of the writing had disappeared. "Some say it was through natural processes—but we Hasidim think differently, quite differently." That's the end of the anecdote, inviting Asher's story to enter the world of legend, and inviting the Hasidim of Khorostkov into MTJ in the twenty-first century.

In the Shiur

On December 23, 2011, my first day in the shiur, I joined about ten or twelve fellows crowded around the conference table in the library. I found a chair a bit back from the table and waited with everyone else for a few minutes. When everyone stood up, I looked up from my Talmud volume to see the Rosh Yeshiva walking in, and stood up as well.

As if I weren't nervous enough already, rather than reviewing the previous discussion, the Rosh Yeshiva immediately began to teach where he had left off the day before. His style is both intimate and matter of fact. He neither pretends to know everything, nor does he proceed as though every word in the Talmud is equally important. ArtScroll may have a precise translation for every word, but the Rosh Yeshiva doesn't—perhaps especially in passages such as those in Gittin that he was teaching when I joined the shiur, which have to do with a range of diseases and the cures, herbal and otherwise, that the rabbis prescribe in that text. At one point he conceded frankly, "These words that appear only once or twice . . . [we're not really sure of their meaning]."

His analytic strategies are designed both to engage deeply with the text of the Gemara and the major commentators Rashi and Tosafos, and to realize when it is time to accept our bafflement and move on. On one occasion, therefore, faced with a puzzle that stumped everyone in the shiur, the Rosh Yeshiva said, "Sometimes you just have to accept it. After you accept it maybe you'll get a *svore* [here, a way to explain the seeming contradiction]." Another day, however, he told us that in fact the Talmud itself wants us to proceed slowly, by trial and error. "Say svores that are no good. [Then say to yourself] 'Oh, it's no good.' But you have to go step by step. That's how the Gemara wants you to work.... If he goes steady like that turtle, he'll catch something, but if he jumps like that rabbit ..."

Nevertheless, where other yeshivas and teachers are famous for the amount of time they will spend on one folio, the Rosh Yeshiva bears in mind the importance of impetus as well. "But let's get a move on—we have Tosafos yet." Another day, after we'd been in shiur for nearly an hour, and reached a natural stopping point just before the next mishnah, he announced as if responding to a demand from someone in the shiur, "Oh, you wanna learn the mishnah, we'll learn the mishnah!" And yet another day, we finished just a couple of minutes before noon, but the Rosh Yeshiva clearly wanted to move further: "Okay, we have a few minutes, and here's some Gemara that doesn't have much Tosafos—we'll learn a little bit."

Of course, the Rosh Yeshiva's is not the only voice in the shiur. Asher and Yisroel Ruven most often serve him as debating foils, pushing very hard sometimes against his proposed solutions, insisting that certain problems in the text get attention. But they can also encourage others to serve in that role. One morning I arrived around 10:00 a.m. to find Asher out. Yisroel Ruven saw me from the library and called out, "vilst lernen?" (Do you want to study together?) Soon after we began, we were joined by his then-current chevrusa, whom I knew well by face but not by name until that moment. The latter posed a question about a certain point in the Gemara's discussion, at the top of Bava Kama 15a, between the respective liabilities of men and women in regard to various categories of infraction.

Yisroel Ruven said, "It's a good question, and if you ask it in shiur, maybe we'll get an interesting answer."

His chevrusa suggested that maybe Yisroel Ruven could ask it in his stead. "Mordechai has an interesting question." Yet upon second thought he wasn't sure this would be a good idea: "Yeah, when you do that, it's always the dumb questions [to which the answer is], 'It's in the *posuk* [verse], nu?'"

Over the course of my kollel year, the hour began to go by much faster for me, and I was rarely in a hurry for it to end—yet still there were days when it felt like the Rosh Yeshiva was wandering in a trackless Tosafos with no one but Yisroel Ruven and Asher even in shouting distance of him. While we were studying the passage in the tractate Sotah that deals with the Israelites' crossing of the Jordan, we spent most of one shiur on a Tosafos at Sotah 34b focusing on the Gemara's term *kekhaniyasan* (as they were encamped). The word as used here refers to the view that the Israelites (that is, the 600,000 adult males) passed through the Jordan exactly in the same formation as they were encamped (the other view is that they passed through one by one). In the view of the Gemara, they all had to be in the Jordan "until everything was finished that the Lord commanded Joshua to speak unto the people" (Joshua 4:10), because the verse says *be'avru*, "as they were crossing," or less literally, "when they crossed" (Joshua 4:7). The Gemara reads that term literally to mean, "while they were still in the Jordan." How could 600,000 male adults have stood in the middle of the river at the same time? Tosafos comment: "nimshekhu ze etsel ze vetsomtsemu" (they were drawn toward each other and reduced), a lovely echo of Jacques Derrida's notion (from *The Animal That Therefore I Am*) of the human condition of "être serrè," to be squished together. At this, someone mentioned the crowding in the Temple at festival time, when the Israelites barely had enough room to stand next to each other but were, miraculously, all able to prostate themselves at the same time. A question that seems within bounds is: Why question how this particular miracle worked, when we simply accept that other comparable miracles worked miraculously? Why, that is, rather than just say "it was a miracle," or alternatively "it's just a metaphor," did the

Rosh Yeshiva lead the shiur in an extended attempt to figure out how this crossing of the Jordan on its dry bed could possibly have taken place, and what that would have required?

The simple answer, as far as the shiur goes, is that Tosafos decided that the calculations were possible and worthwhile. In a somewhat skeptical mode, I noted in my diary: "This Tosafos is a wonderful item for Christian charges of Jewish literalism—and it's also great fun." Moreover, I would guess with a high degree of confidence that Christian contemporaries of the Tosafists were similarly interested in working out the mathematics of miracles. Is that what the famous question about how many angels can dance on the head of a pin, lehavdil, is really about?

Willing as he is to devote time to the attempt to comprehend Tosafos together with everyone in the shiur, the Rosh Yeshiva also from time to time expresses his frustration with the difficulties this medieval commentary presents for us. After puzzling for some time over a Tosafos about whether a certain logical inference could have been drawn from target to source rather than from source to target, he declared: "Tosafos had a shortage of paper [and therefore wrote in telegraphic style] and if he didn't have a shortage of paper [it would be so long that] we wouldn't read it anyway. . . . This Tosafos is for Tosafos." Another time his frustration was aimed at the later commentators on Tosafos, rather than on the Tosafists themselves. Finding nothing in these commentators on a particular point (end of Tosafos, Bava Kama 55b, beginning with the word *ileymo*), he complained, "When you need them they're not there. When you don't need them they give you every *pshat* [straightforward gloss]."

Another passage of entirely remarkable calculations, a few folios later in the same tractate, did provoke an explanation by the Rosh Yeshiva. Sotah 37 includes a discussion among the rabbis of how many *britot* (covenants) were made between the Jews (counted individually for this purpose) and God—three moments of covenant, times 613 commandments, times 48 facets for each commandment (do and don't, general and particular, etc.), times 603,550 males, and so forth. The total seemed astronomical. As we filed out, Yisroel Ruven's chevrusa asked the Rosh Yeshiva, "What's the point of all this?"

The Rosh Yeshiva replied: "It's trying to scare you—you think a mitzvah is just a mitzvah?"—on the contrary, each of the 613 mitzvos contains a multitude.

We resumed the discussion the next day. The calculations of the number of mitzvos, which I still didn't quite follow, seemed to be about 17,758,000,000. Yisroel Ruven's chevrusa worked it all out on an Excel spreadsheet that he kindly e-mailed to me.

Through all this, I make rough attempts to gauge my own progress. The shiur itself moves and stalls, moves and circles. For me, part of the impulse to come to the yeshiva, rather than only continue studying on my own with the ArtScroll elucidation as I'd been doing for years, was to learn how to learn Gemara in the old-fashioned way, studying every comment by Rashi and Tosafos, and with no English in front of me. Of course, even with ArtScroll, the texts can seem complex and opaque. But generally, the commentary provided in that edition (largely reliant on Rashi whenever possible) creates something of the illusion of a straightforward, coherent text. That is, from ArtScroll alone one would never conceive the problems posited especially by Tosafos, who sought to reconcile (for the first time, as some scholars argue) divergent statements throughout the Babylonian Talmud, thus making it into a coherent "book" rather than a rabbinic anthology.

One afternoon in January 2012, I noted, "I was quite lost by the end of the shiur today, in a Tosafos dealing with a complex question of the effects of a conditional *get* [bill of divorce] that might be retroactive but whose retroactivity has in any case not kicked in yet." I can still get easily lost years later. On the other hand, at least I've been learning how to *read* Rashi and Tosafos; comprehension is beginning to come now too, years later, as I puzzle how to turn my experiences into a book.

Especially at the very beginning, I noticed that my training in secular legal scholarship helped me to participate in discussions before and after the shiur. I came out of one especially long shiur while we were still in the tractate Gittin with the impression that while foreseeable or relatively common forms of death will validate a *get* (bill of divorce) that a man proffers to his wife on condition that "I die from this disease" or "I don't recover from this disease," uncommon and unforeseeable accidents (a lion ate the husband, or the house fell on him) are not, since we cannot reasonably expect that he was contemplating such uncommon accidents. Gavriel Pinsker was, like me, one of the last to leave the room. He turned to me: "So Silverstein, with the Twin Towers—he got his money, even though it was an 'act of God,' right?" I said, "Right, that's the term they use in civil law for *ones d'lo shchiach,*" an extraordinary accident.

Another distinction familiar to lawyers—between the logical force of an argument and the force it may gain from being vociferously propounded—also came up at least once. The term *ne'eneh* appeared when we reached Gittin 83a. The determination has been made, over the course of the few folios preceding Gittin 83a, that the halacha is according to the view of Rabbi Eliezer: If a man says to his wife, "You are [divorced from me and] permitted to every man [on condition that you do not marry] Mr. X," this is a valid divorce. After Rabbi Eliezer's death, four great Tannaim, scholars of the mishnaic era, attempt to refute that ruling. Each one's reasoning is listed in turn, with the formula "*ne'eneh* Rabbi Y——." I would have thought that *ne'eneh* simply means "answered," but the Rosh Yeshiva indicated that this term indicates speaking loudly or shouting (someone joked that this is because Rabbi Eliezer is dead but they're still trying to argue with him). He suggested that they spoke loudly because their arguments were weak. "The louder you shout, the weaker your arguments are. Yeah, they were shouting. [As if to say] I know you [Rabbi Eliezer, ruling that a declaration of divorce barring the wife from marrying one specified individual is nevertheless valid] are wrong, but I can't prove it to you!"

When I was working as a lawyer, I heard the formula go this way: "If the law is on your side, pound on the law. If the facts are on your side, pound on the facts. If neither the facts nor the law is on your side, pound on the table!"

And occasionally—but really just *very* occasionally, it seemed—I was able to speak up and make a tentative contribution to the shiur's deliberations. At the very end of my kollel year, we were deep in a discussion in Sotah 34a about the spies whom Moses sent out to reconnoiter the Land of Israel before the decision was taken to attempt its conquest. The spies brought back a bunch of grapes from the Land that was so large "they carried it upon a pole between two" (Numbers 13:23). There Rabbi Yitzkhok (at least in Rashi's reading) argues that the bunch of grapes brought back by the spies was carried on four poles by eight spies, although the simplest reading seems to be one pole carried by two spies. Rabbi Yitzkhok's disputants, as usual collectively referred to simply as "the rabbis," agree that there were at least two poles. Rashi's view is disputed by another very early commentator, Rabbenu Chananel, who apparently suggests that Rabbi Yitzkhok is arguing that there were just two poles, but carried by a total of eight men. Assuming, however, Rashi's reading is correct, Rabbi Yitzkhok's view that there were four poles seems to follow from his presumption that the grapes were carried by eight. I spoke up and suggested, "Rebbi, couldn't it be from the language: 'veyisa'uhu bemot beshnayim' (they carried it on a stick by two), since *veyisa'uhu* is plural, *bemot* is two [the rabbis have established that a pole is always carried by two] and *beshnayim* is two, so two times two times two is eight?"

He heard me and said, "Yeah, the Gemara does that sometimes."

Yisroel Ruven added sotto voce, to me, not as a rebuke but as a kind of amplification or clarification of the Rosh Yeshiva's response: "But it didn't do it here."

Around the winter of 2013, I noticed a passage in the Gemara (Bava Kama 14a, on the bottom) that contained a reading that seems very forced. Quoting a *baraisa* (a tannaitic text not included in the Mishnah), the Gemara there reads "not to this one and not to that one" to mean "only to one of them [in this case, the one who was damaged]." This sounds puzzling because it is: "not to this one and not to that one" should mean "to neither one of them." I spoke up, loudly, and got the Rosh Yeshiva's attention: How can you read it that way? It seems very forced.

The Rosh Yeshiva responded, "God made it come out in a way that's going to make us work hard to understand it right."

What underlay my question is a perception that I couldn't quite articulate in shiur, both because of its complexity and because I was worried it might take a step beyond the bounds of acceptable discourse on the status of the talmudic text, although I did articulate it to Nasanel later. In its original formulation in the baraisa, the statement "neither this one's nor that one's" works very well, since the baraisa is running through four possible relations between the location where a certain occasion of damage takes place, and the question of who is liable for that damage. That is, the damage can take place at (1) the damager's property; (2) the damaged party's property; (3) a shared space; or (4) a space that belongs to neither of them. This makes it especially difficult to say just that "the Tannaim were speaking loosely" in this case, since it seems that the baraisa quite precisely really wants to cover all four possibilities. The difficulty is that within the larger context of this chapter in Bava Kama, the categories of liability under discussion here—that caused by an ox's "tooth" on one hand, and by its "foot" on the other—only apply in "the field of another," where "the field of another" is taken in turn to mean the field of the damaged party. Hence, a space that belongs to neither of them would be a space void of the potential for liability of either party.

I couldn't help thinking the thought that I partially censored, the one that seems to exceed the universe of the yeshiva. It does not seem that the language of the baraisa is loose. Rather there are two possibilities, either one of them threatening to the authority of the Tannaim and to the coherence of the entire talmudic text that students have been working to establish at least since the time of Tosafos. One possibility is that, for the sake of formal completeness, the baraisa is including a "possibility" that is legally meaningless. The other possibility is that the baraisa is referring to a different set of rules, where (for example) "tooth" and "foot" may incur liability in a field that is private property of a third party—a clear impossibility as these categories are conventionally understood. This implies, however, that even "correct" or "validated" baraisos might refer to legal orders different from those implicit in the Mishnah and elaborated by the Gemara. These were not, it seemed to me, thoughts to articulate in the shiur, which operates according to the rule that ultimately all tannaitic literature is part of one system, even though different segments of that literature may vary in degree of authority and even accuracy.

On another occasion I did receive at least a hint that the human production of parts of Scripture might be taken into account, at least in private deliberations in the beis medresh. A discussion at the bottom of Sotah 35a mentions that David was punished because he said, in the words of a Psalm, "your statutes were *zemiros* [songs] to me." The Gemara explains David's sin: "Words of Torah, about which it is written 'Close your eyes and it is gone' [Proverbs 23:5]"—that is, that are very difficult—you treat as lightly as a song?

Hillel noted: "Didn't King Solomon write Proverbs?" This would create a problem for the Gemara's assertion putting these words in the mouth of King David, since in effect he would have been quoting a text written later, by his own son.

Asher: "I think so."

Hillel: "So it's funny that God is quoting it against King David."

Me: "Just because the son wrote it down doesn't mean the father didn't know it."

Asher: "Yeah, it was probably things that were . . ."

The reason this exchange intrigued me was because I knew (I think) what I was doing with my invocation of the idea that texts predate their recording—I was drawing on my (secular) knowledge that parts of the Bible began as oral texts, but using that knowledge to defend the coherence of the talmudic text.

So if I made a bit of progress in my studies, one way of marking it was the ability to know what kinds of intervention might be appropriate in what situations. Some of my progress, too, was simply in getting to know and hence anticipate the Rosh Yeshiva's style. On the last day of 2013, I was sorry to have to leave early and miss the shiur. I knew we were going to cover the Gemara that asserts that lions pounce on their prey and eat it, and do not normally kill it first. I'd heard the Rosh Yeshiva talk about animals—either in themselves, or as hypothetical figures deployed in the give-and-take of the Gemara, and told Asher it would be fun to hear his explanation of this putative leonine behavior. When I came in the next morning, Asher said to me, "You were right—the Rebbi had a great time describing this. He explained that when the lion tears a limb off the animal that's his prey, it can still scream, and that's music for the lion. And that's the way a king [the lion as the king of animals] eats its dinner—with music."

The main challenges of Gemara study are logical and philological: understanding how to parse this unpunctuated text, recalling the tannaitic statements that the Gemara tries to reconcile or to draw upon in hermeneutic debates, following the strategies of arguments that become familiar after years of study. Yet there is often room for ethical concerns to be raised as well, and these are not out of place in the shiur. Of all the participants in the shiur, Yisroel Ruven is also the one most likely to protest a talmudic dictum on the grounds of something like a universal logic or ethics. Early on in my kollel year, we were studying (at Gittin 71b) the status of deaf-mutes vis-à-vis two facets of family law. One was their capacity to be married and divorced; these they can do. The other, as I've mentioned above, follows somewhat different standards and addresses their capacity to participate in the rituals of yibum (the levirate marriage) and chalitzah (renunciation of yibum); they can do the first, which only requires a physical act, but not the latter, which requires speech. This leads to the following conundrum: Can a deaf-mute whose brother dies be divorced from his brother's widow, after he becomes her new husband through yibum? That is, certainly he can marry her, but perhaps he cannot then sever the bond? The answer: If the deceased brother had been fully able, and thus his original marriage to the woman who is now a widow was fully valid according to biblical law, the deaf-mute surviving brother cannot effectively divorce his wife after taking her in yibum. By stepping into his deceased brother's shoes as the widow's husband through the yibum ceremony, he has likewise become fully married to her on the biblical level, but is only capable of divorce at the lower rabbinic level. Thus, if the surviving deaf-mute brother leaves the widow (now his wife through yibum), she's stuck, a grass widow, an *agunah*. Perhaps, the Gemara suggests in the course of the discussion, this ban should be extended to the case where there were two brothers, both deaf-mutes, one now deceased, and the other in position to perform the levirate marriage with his deaf-mute brother's widow. On one hand, even the first marriage was only valid rabbinically and not at the level of biblical law, and therefore we might say that rabbinic divorce suffices for the second marriage to be validly ended. On the other, perhaps we "decree" that even in this case the divorce is impossible, lest people think that it can be done even where the deceased brother was fully able and the first marriage biblically valid.

Yisroel Ruven objected: "How could the rabbis create new *agunahs* [abandoned wives] like that?" That is, why would the rabbis want to institute a rule that was bad for innocent people—in this case, the hapless widows of deaf-mutes, who can never be freed from their marriage bond?

The Rosh Yeshiva's first answer was categorical: "It's true, *derakheho darkhey noam vekol nesivoseho shalom* [the Torah's ways are ways of pleasantness and all of its paths are peace, Proverbs 3:17]. But there are exceptions. We don't know what they were thinking, but there are exceptions."

Later it turned out that this "decree" of the rabbis was only hypothetical. The final ruling is that in fact, the deaf-mute husband of a deaf-mute brother's widow can indeed divorce her (but

don't rely on me, ask your local Orthodox rabbi). "See," the Rosh
Yeshiva chuckled, "the Gemara doesn't even go that way. He
[Yisroel Ruven] is complaining about a *hava amina* [hypotheti-
cal]," and not an actual ruling of the rabbis.

At the end of a shiur late in 2013, the Rosh Yeshiva was inspired
by a bit of Tosafos (on Bava Kama 14b) to discuss manuscript
history.

> Tosafos only had a few copies of the Gemara. In those days, if
> you wanted a set of the Talmud, you went to somebody who
> had one and you copied it from him. Or maybe there was some-
> one who copied them for a living: "If you want a copy, I can
> make you one." But anyway, people didn't have a lot of books.
> Even a couple of hundred years ago, they didn't have books like
> we have today. The [great twentieth-century authority known
> as the] Chazon Ish says sometimes [in his writings], "I heard
> about an opinion in some sefer, and I don't think I agree with
> it, but I can't say any more because I don't have it." The Chazon
> Ish didn't have it!
>
> [And if they were copying all this by hand, mistakes came
> into the copies.] And it's not only in the Oral Torah—it's in
> Scripture already. [The text called] Masechet Sofrim, which is
> from the Tannaim already, says they came to a point where they
> had different variants, they didn't know which was the original,
> and they decided by majority vote. *Akharey harabim lehatos*
> [you shall determine according to the majority]. . . . That's why
> it says, "He gave the Torah to His people Israel." What do you
> mean He gave it to us—He doesn't have it anymore? He can't
> learn it at the same time? No: it means He gave it to us and now
> it's ours, as we say it is. *Ay*, it's full of [discrepancies]? So He
> makes a lot of *hagahos* [emendations] in His own copy!

This much, or most of it, seems to be the Rosh Yeshiva's citation
from the eighteen-century sage known as the Vilna Gaon. The
Rosh Yeshiva continues:

But it's all intended that way, including the changes—that's how God wants the Torah to be. If it was changed to read *lo sivashel gedi bekhaylev imo* [do not cook a kid in the fat of its mother] instead of *bekholov imo* [the milk of its mother], then we wouldn't need to separate *milchig* [dairy] and *fleishig* [meat], we could throw out our two sets of dishes—we'd just have to be careful not to cook a goat in its mother's fat.

[And it still happens now, with printing.] The first edition of [the Rosh Yeshiva's own version of the Passover Haggadah known as] *Kol dodi* came out with an instruction in English, "They each dip their finger in the blood." The blood—instead of the wine. We corrected it, but that's how the first printing came out.[2]

Yisroel Ruven: "It's the blood libel, Rebbi!"

The Rosh Yeshiva (laughing, as he stands up to end the shiur): "It's the blood libel."

4

Rebbi

AS REFLECTED in this book, the leader of our shiur is almost never addressed as "you," but rather referred to either as "the Rosh Yeshiva" or as "Rebbi," a term broadly used in Ashkenazic Jewish culture to refer to any teacher of Torah, from one who instructs small children to the most advanced lecturers. This honorific is often used in his absence—and even, as occasionally happens, when the interlocutor is expressing frustration over the attempt to reach a shared understanding of a difficult text. The latter term especially, with its basic connotation of the teacher's role, also suggests that this is one from whom disciples can learn not only the right way to study the text, but also a sound sense of being Jewish in the world. I catch glimpses of what that sound sense of being might constitute in fleeting moments, either those I observe or those that others recollect so that I may be instructed in turn.

Unlike the paradigmatic hasidic leader, similarly addressed and referred to as "the Rebbe," our Rebbi's authority is, if anything, anticharismatic and reserved. He has not striven to build a community of devoted followers, but rather serves the community as it happens to manifest itself (and, to the extent that his community is geographically designated as the Orthodox population of the Lower East Side, as it seems to grow gradually but steadily smaller). One day I overheard Asher reply to someone: "That's so not like Rebbi. Rebbi, if he sees someone doing something he disagrees with, he won't say anything. But if you come to him and try to justify it, he'll throw the book at you." And during the week that the Lower East Side was without power after Hurricane Sandy, Elissa and I took refuge with cousins in Washington Heights, and were kindly invited to Shabbes meals at the homes of local residents there. Another guest at dinner that Friday night was a young man named Yehoshua who clearly had a yeshivish background, and was pursuing a master's degree in art history at Bard while working at the Cloisters. He told us had spent some time at MTJ during his high school years. In response to my comment about how remarkable it is to be in a small room with just about ten other guys listening to a shiur by one of the top halachic authorities of our generation, he told me he believed the Rosh Yeshiva had stayed on the Lower East Side precisely because he doesn't want to be the object of mass veneration.

The Judge

Our custom is to be in the room before the Rebbi enters, and to stand upon his entry. One day (just that once, to my recollection) Yisroel Ruven, sensing the Rebbi was about to come in, intoned: "All rise." I had mentioned to Asher months earlier that, when the Rosh Yeshiva walks toward the front of the beis medresh for minchah with his big black hat, he looks like the judge in an old Western movie.

At least once I heard the Rebbi wonder aloud about the source of his own authority. One day we worked through a very long Tosafos (at Sotah 24) that took up the full hour. The Rebbi introduced this text by saying, "Today we have a Tosafos that has nothing to do" with the ostensible topic of the passage in the Gemara to which it is attached as commentary. Rather, this discussion turned on the fundamental principle of rabbinic biblical interpretation that nothing is superfluous in the Torah—and that therefore, every seeming superfluity is available to teach us something not explicitly stated in the text. On the other hand, the Gemara will also sometimes claim that at certain points, rather than redundancies being available for interpretation, the Torah is merely "speaking in human language," as people would in conversation. Insofar as I followed the thread, Tosafos spends a good deal of words establishing the following propositions:

(a) Each of several key Tannaim, such as Rabbi Meir, sometimes argues that *dibra Torah* (the Torah spoke) in the manner of human speech, and since humans often speak in redundancies, therefore nothing is to be learned from redundancies, while at other times each of the same Tannaim does interpret redundancies;

(b) the argument among them seems to be rather whether redundancies can teach something extraneous to the context of the redundant phrase itself; however,

(c) another Tanna, Rabbi Akiva, does seem to believe that *all* redundancies teach something novel and can never be simply dismissed with the notion of the Torah speaking in human language.

Along the way, the Rosh Yeshiva several times worried the question of the seeming arbitrariness of the principle's being applied sometimes and not others: "How do we *know* this one is *dibra toyre*, and that one is something we interpret? Because his Rebbi told him! But who told his Rebbi? So is it all ultimately *halachos lemoshe misinai* [laws orally dictated to Moses and not actually derivable from Scripture]? And if so, then these are all just *asmachtos* [proof texts for citation, but not the actual sources of the law]?"

He did not answer his own question, on this occasion—but he did on another. The Rebbi commented on a series of very general proof texts presented (at Sotah 23b) for why certain rules pertain to male kohanim and not to daughters of kohanim, and certain rules pertain to men generally and not to women: "Don't try to interpret the verses too closely—they're very general. It's all really *halacha lemoshe misinai* and the rabbis were just trying to convince the masses. You could spend five days trying to read it precisely, and you'd really be wasting your time. You should keep studying the text further instead." Yet Asher had earlier that same morning quoted the Rebbi to almost the opposite effect: the Rebbi had once quoted the scholar known as Malbim, to the effect that if we really knew Hebrew grammar properly, we would understand why all of the proof texts the rabbis cite are compelling.

The Rosh Yeshiva is able to raise these issues, it appears to me, at least in part due to his conviction (stated in other contexts) that we do know in fact what the halacha, the proper Jewish procedure, is, whether or not we are absolutely certain of its particular source in the text. Related to this conviction is his penchant for attempting to make sense of the talmudic text, in the standard "Vilna edition," as it is printed, before considering the various emendations that have been suggested over recent centuries and that are duly marked in that same edition. Thus, in a Tosafos as printed at Sotah 25b, the word *ve'ayno*, "and he does not," is left out in a quote from the Gemara elsewhere, so that the entire meaning of the quoted Gemara is obscured. While we were sitting in the library waiting for the Rebbi, several of us noted this. Someone said, "Should we tell the Rosh Yeshiva about it?"

Asher: "No, because maybe he'll come up with a *pshat* [a way to make sense of the text as printed], and we would have missed it if we told him."

In fact, the Rosh Yeshiva puzzled over it for a few seconds, then said, "maybe it's a mistake."

A conversation at the yeshiva, one Shabbes afternoon when I had just returned to New York after a good three weeks in Ithaca, further illustrated for me the Rosh Yeshiva's dedication to making sense of the text on his own as far as possible. I arrived a few minutes late for minchah, and was pleased to see Yisroel Ruven there. I asked him how the shiur had been going, and he told me that they'd gotten stuck on a difficult Rashi at Bava Kama 65b. I said, "Do you want to show it to me?" and so had the unusual pleasure of sitting and learning with Yisroel Ruven for a solid half hour or so before the evening service and the end of Shabbes.

The general issue is whether and under what circumstances a thief must make restitution according to the value of the stolen item at the time it was stolen, or at the time of judgement or valuation, if its value has risen or fallen in the meantime. Rashi introduces a distinction that does not seem to be based on any indications or difficulties in the Gemara. I asked Yisroel Ruven if any of the commentators "at the back" (of the Gemara) deals with this, and he said, "Oh yeah," indicating a few authorities, including the *Dibros Moshe*. He explained to me, "That's Reb Moshe Feinstein's commentary on the Gemara. He cites Rishonim, Acharonim, various Gemaras—it's funny, his style is completely different from the Rosh Yeshiva's. We tried to read the Gemara in a way that would make clear why Rashi had to make that distinction, but we just couldn't come up with anything." Yisroel Ruven seemed to be suggesting that, by contrast, our Rosh Yeshiva heavily emphasizes trying to make sense of the text on our own, certainly before and often to the exclusion of consulting later authorities.

Perhaps the Rosh Yeshiva is willing to accept a certain degree of necessary misapprehension of the rabbinic texts because of his conviction that *the halacha for us is what we do*. A different time, while ultimately acceding to an emendation, he insisted it was not necessary although it produced an assertion directly contrary to the text as it stands: "Okay, you can do like the *Bach* and take out the word *lo* [not] here, and that makes it easier to interpret. But we could also interpret it the other way. It wouldn't change the halacha, because we know what the halacha is, because the halacha is what we do."

Such an assertion seems to reflect a striking confidence in the integrity of a tradition of halachic practice as handed down to us. The term here is *minhag*, as noted above, not in perhaps its most common sense of "custom" as opposed to "law," but rather as the authorized version of practice for a given community. Asher told me of someone who had studied at the famous Yeshiva Torah Vodaath in Brooklyn, who tried to dispute the Rebbi on a particular point of halacha. The disputant "brought a sefer [a printed authority] to show how the halacha should be, and the Rebbi shouted, 'You're going to start *paskening* [deciding the law] from seforim now? That's not our minhag!'"[1]

When he told me this story I demurred: "But how do we know what our minhag is?"

Asher was not willing to concede the point. "We do know what the minhag is! Reb Moshe [Feinstein] got it from the Vilna Gaon, who got it from the Rishonim! Don't say we don't know what the minhag is anymore!"

The notion of minhag as "the halacha that applies to us" was also pertinent to a rich interaction I had one day with Rabbi Goldman and the Mashgiach. Rabbi Goldman and I were then studying the *Beis Yosef*'s commentary to the first chapter of the *Tur* in *Even haezer*, the volume that deals with issues pertinent to marriage and family law. That first chapter concerns in particular the ramifications of the famous *herem* (here meaning an edict on pain of excommunication) attributed to Rabbenu Gershom (born in Metz, 960), which forbade Jewish men from having more than one wife at a time—and as a crucial corollary, also declared that Jewish women could not be divorced against their will. I hadn't known about the latter part of the herem, or hadn't consciously considered it, and I was intrigued by the notion that a wife could refuse to accept a *get* (bill of divorce) and thereby leave her husband hanging.

According to the *Beis Yosef*, there is at least one case in which a wife can be given an effective get whether she accepts it or not. This case is where she has converted to another religion. The procedure is to appoint someone to receive the get on her behalf, on the grounds that it is actually in her own interest for her to be divorced rather than to commit adultery as a married woman.

I asked Rabbi Goldman whether this question of the "stuck" husband—prevented from remarrying by his wife's refusal to accept the get—ever came up today. He proposed asking the Mashgiach, which was great for me because it finally gave me something to ask the Mashgiach about. The Mashgiach's first response was to gently challenge Rabbi Goldman: "Why are you asking me whether this of all things is something we still do today? Didn't that question come up about anything earlier [in the section of the *Tur* we were studying]?" Then I explained that it was really my question: I wanted to know if there were really such cases. The Mashgiach responded that there are such cases, but they don't get much sympathy or publicity, because (unlike the case of women whose husbands refuse to offer a get) in the case of men whose wives refuse to divorce them, there is a way to get around Rabbenu Gershom's ban on a man's divorcing his wife against her will. That workaround is the *heter meah* (release by a hundred), a declaration signed by a hundred rabbis from at least three countries that the woman is not in her proper mind and thus the requirement of her voluntary acceptance is waived.

> But a heter meah isn't an easy thing to do, and it can be done improperly as well. And also, it doesn't take away the herem—it just holds it off. There's a story about the [former] Rosh Yeshiva [Reb Moshe Feinstein] that someone was looking for a heter meah, and the husband's uncle was very involved in the effort. They finally got it from some rabbi, and they consulted Reb Moshe about it, and he said it was improper. Then the guy's uncle died an unnatural death. They came to Reb Moshe and said, "You killed him [the uncle]." Reb Moshe said, "I didn't kill him. Rabbenu Gershom killed him."

Rabbenu Gershom's herem was said to have been originally issued only for a limited time—a stipulation that, according to the commentators, was necessary in order not to transgress the prohibition against "adding" to the precepts of the Torah. The Mashgiach told us, "It was extended, although I don't think we know exactly by whom, and certainly they weren't such *gedolim* [luminaries] as Rabbenu Gershom." He added that Rabbenu Gershom probably thought no extension would be needed, since no one in Rabbenu Gershom's time imagined that the Messiah would take so long. "That's caused lots of problems."

Rabbi Goldman also wanted to know about a related issue in the same chapter of the *Tur*: the requirement for a man to divorce his wife if they are still childless after ten years. The Mashgiach said, "It's not our minhag to do that. We stay married anyway."

But Rabbi Goldman wanted to know, "The Gemara explicitly says you have to do it [go through with such a divorce]. How can we ignore that?"

The Mashgiach: "If it's not our minhag, we don't do it. The Gemara also says we should light Chanukah candles outside, but we don't do that, right?" Then he added a story about an exchange of letters between the late Rabbi Elyashiv, a "Lithuanian" scholar who lived in Israel, and Rabbi Ehrenzweig ("a Galicianer," meaning that his family were from the former Austro-Hungarian province of Galicia). Rabbi Elyashiv explained that the reason why we light candles inside now is because of "danger" (from the Gentiles) outside of the Land of Israel. Rabbi Ehrenzweig replied, "If you can say that, then you obviously never lived outside of the Land of Israel: 'In Cracow, the whole neighborhood was Jewish. The Gentiles never came in, and if they did come in, they weren't interested in our candles.'"

Further on the question of forced divorce, the Mashgiach pointed, as had Rabbi Goldman, to the example of the great twentieth-century scholar known as the Chazon Ish, who even while living in the Land of Israel, did not divorce his barren wife. "It's not our minhag; we do not compel the divorce now. Whatever the reasons, the minhag was established." He suggested it might have had to do with historical circumstances in which a Jew, once divorced, might have been prevented by the civil authorities from remarrying: "Better to stay married [than to risk not being able to marry again]." The bottom line: that's our minhag now, whatever the Gemara says, and that's the way we do it.

"So," asked Rabbi Goldman, "if someone came to a rabbi now and said, 'We've been married ten years and we don't have any children, should I divorce my wife?' What would the rabbi say?"

The Mashgiach replied that actually, "some rabbi might even say today that he should divorce her, but it's wrong—it's not our minhag."

This rhetorically firm reliance on minhag does not imply a folkloric or "customary" mode of Jewishness, but rather a grounding of authoritative practice in the community's historically contingent adaptation of its practice in areas with legal significance. I suspect strongly that it is closely interdependent with what I consider another distinctive feature of MTJ—the remarkable degree of freedom of speech or thought within the boundaries of observed traditional practice. Doctrinal policing, that is, may be less rigorously enforced in a community that is less anxious about what its members are actually doing—precisely because what its members are doing is "our minhag."

Freedom is also manifest in our beis medresh through the discretion that each participant exercises in deciding whether to attend the Rebbi's shiurim, to study the same texts without attending, or to concentrate on entirely different texts. This is quite different from most yeshivas, where the course of study is strictly determined, either for everyone at the yeshiva or group by group. It hasn't always been so, as I learned one day when our shiur reached folio 51b of Bava Kama. The principle of *breirah* arose. In the case at point, the term here, according to its usual meaning, would have meant that ownership of a certain item would have become fixed permanently at some recent time, but only determined retrospectively. Yet, the Rosh Yeshiva pointed out, here the principle seemed inapposite, as it was being used idiosyncratically, to imply vacillating ownership. "If you don't take my question into account, the Gemara works perfectly."

At the end of the shiur, he referred us to a long commentary by the fourteenth-century Reb Nissim of Gerona (the "Ran") on the topic. At my urging, Asher, Hillel, and I turned to that Ran after shiur. Asher mentioned the experience of having studied the tractate Nedarim (vows) at MTJ, since for that tractate the Ran's commentary takes the place usually occupied by Rashi. The

Mashgiach, newly arrived himself, had decided with the Rosh Ye-shiva's permission that everyone should be studying the same trac-tate. Asher says he was against the idea: "Here's a yeshiva where I can finally learn my own way, and they want to make it like every other yeshiva?" The regime lasted through two tractates, Nedarim and Sukkah, and then reverted to the controlled autonomy we see today.

More Moments

Perhaps the most common form in which impressions of a promi-nent rabbinic teacher are passed down is the brief oral vignette. It seems right therefore to conclude this chapter, focusing on our Rebbi as a figure of authority, with a series of such vignettes as I observed them or as they were passed down to me—and, as throughout this book, with a minimum of the kind of analysis and commentary that usually mark professional anthropology.

Bug Scare

At the end of the shiur, Yisroel Ruven shows the Rosh Yeshiva a flyer that had been posted on the door of the beis medresh, under the letterhead of the Chicago Rabbinical Council. The flyer an-nounces that there has been a higher incidence of bugs in barley, and therefore every bag of barley has to be checked entirely, not just part of it. Yisroel Ruven asked, "Is that the yeshiva's policy?" The Rosh Yeshiva answered, "It'll catch on in a few weeks, and then it'll die out. These things have a life-span of six weeks." I wasn't sure what he meant by "these things." At first it seemed to me that he was referring to the concern about kashrut itself, and suggesting that it might be merely an example of overzealousness. Writing now—over five years later—it seems more likely to me that he was referring to the bugs themselves as having a short life-span. In other words, while the rabbinical concern may have been justified, we could presume that the issue that provoked that concern would shortly be obviated. If I'm correct, this was an example of the Rosh Yeshiva's ability to respect other legal opinions without necessarily requiring a change in the practice of those who follow his own authority.

The Primacy of Logic

Asher passes on to me a remark by the Rosh Yeshiva in shiur, which Asher said he only understood after listening to it several times on the recording Asher faithfully makes. At a certain point the Gemara derives the meaning of a term from its use in another context, but the Gemara itself goes on to wonder, "What did we need that for—we could have figured it out through our own logical deduction!" Now, it would seem that scriptural authority is stronger than our own human rational powers. On the contrary, the Rosh Yeshiva's point, if I'm conveying Asher's understanding accurately here, was precisely that a logical deduction of the meaning is actually a stronger proof than learning it from the context of another verse. As Asher put it: "*svore* is the *posek*"—"logic is the verse," or more loosely and hence more precisely, deduction is the primary source for this point, while the scriptural source is secondary.

The Oral and the Written

One day the shiur ended with a story about talebearers being punished by having worms come out of their tongues, go into their stomach, and back. The Rebbi had signaled the end of the session by closing his Gemara, but hadn't yet stood up to leave the room. Someone took the occasion to ask about a story told about his father Reb Moshe, while still in Luban. According to my rough notes, "Someone came to [Reb Moshe] with his tongue distended; in his dream he had spoken *loshen hora* [said derogatory things] about Lot's daughters." (Later, Asher clarified the anecdote for me. Apparently this was a case of tongue cancer; the person had

spoken ill of Lot's daughters and then they had come to him in a
dream to say he would be punished for it.) At first the Rosh Yeshiva
just said, "I never heard the story." Later he added, "In its essence
it's true, but its details [may be embroidered]. You know, stories
can have babies, too." A few minutes later, while I was in the library with Nasanel looking for a place to study, someone had the
Igros Moshe, the compendium of Reb Moshe Feinstein's respona,
open to the eighth volume, which includes an unsigned bio-
graphical sketch of Reb Moshe. At page 15 of this entry, there's a
version of the story. So was the person looking for this story
checking to see whether the version in the *Igros Moshe* was the
same as the one we'd just heard from our Rosh Yeshiva? And if
they were discrepant, how would he decide which one was more
accurate?

Understanding the Law

Very, very occasionally, my diligent self-study of the ArtScroll
Gemara is rewarded with a gleam of new comprehension of an
allusion that I noticed in the Rebbi's shiur but didn't understand
at the time. During my kollel year, I noted the Rebbi saying, "It
can't be the law—we don't understand it. How can it be the law if
you don't understand it?," which struck me as powerful, beautiful,
and radical at the time. Some two years later, in mid-December 2014,
I found what might have been his source in the Gemara, at Bava
Basra 107b, where Rav Ashi says: "If we do not understand the
reasoning of 'others,' can we decide the halacha in accordance with
their view?"

That same week, the Rosh Yeshiva closed the shiur, and our
extended discussion of a Tosafos, by declaring, "Okay, it's too
technical, we don't understand it." I showed Asher my source in
Bava Basra 107b, and reminded him what the Rebbi had said in
2012. In return, he gave me another story that corroborated the
idea that we must understand a ruling in order to follow it: Once
he had been discussing with the Rosh Yeshiva the dispute between

two Orthodox authorities, both resident in the Holy Land, about how to treat the international date line for various halachic purposes. On the one hand, Rabbi Dushinsky's arguments seemed to make more sense. On the other hand, we always *pasken* (rule in practice) according to the view of the Chazon Ish. But if we don't understand the Chazon Ish, how can we pasken like him? So the ruling is that the actual halacha is left in doubt.

The idea that we can only follow a law that we understand is powerful, beautiful, and radical, but probably unworkable in any real-world society, and hence it's not surprising that the Rosh Yeshiva will also sometimes express the contrary idea: that we have to take rulings on authority. One day toward the end of the shiur, in response to some expressions of consternation at the odd turn the discussion of possible stipulations attached to a divorce had taken, he said, "You know that the Gemara says: 'If you don't understand the Gemara, it's not the end of the world.'" Thus, in the ebb and flow of a teaching practice that is centered on the close reading and interpretation of texts that are authoritative but by no means monological, assertions of our own autonomous responsibility for judgement at one point can coexist with assertions of our obligation to submit to greater (or at least antecedent) authority at others. While this may seem a "contradiction," it does not disable the teaching in practice, and may in fact be the most effective way to sustain a community that is intellectually agile and energetic, but whose fundamental loyalty to Torah as the word of God and a blueprint for Jewish life remains axiomatic.

At Bava Kama 53a, the Gemara quotes an opinion of the Tanna Rabbi Nassan concerning the assignment of liability in a case where an ox is pushed into a pit by another ox. The Gemara finds Rabbi Nassan's opinion (which seems to turn on the distinction in liability between a "first offender" ox and a "repeat offender" ox) internally contradictory. In response to the challenge there, the Gemara quotes the sage known as Rava: "Rabbi Nassan was a *dayan* [a judge in a rabbinical court], and he reaches the profundities of the law." The Gemara then goes on to elaborate two rationales for Rabbi Nassan's view, prefaced with the term le'oylem, best translated here as "Actually." Given the lack of punctuation in the Gemara, it is impossible to tell for sure whether the two rationales are stated in the name of Rava or not. When we finished reading through those two rationales, the Rebbi said a bit sardonically, "Congratulations, you're all dayanim now."

That day I was joined in the shiur by a visiting Israeli Talmudist. He heard the Rosh Yeshiva to read the Gemara's comment that "Rabbi Nassan was a judge" as a sarcastic remark about Rabbi Nassan's "profundity." This reading is strengthened if we take the following le'oylem as introducing the Gemara's own defense against a dismissive remark by Rava—that is, if we read it as saying, in effect, "Rava was unconvinced by Rabbi Nassan's argument even though Rabbi Nassan had a lofty title . . . but actually Rabbi Nassan's argument has merit." Moreover, the Rebbi's "Congratulations" reminded me of something he had said perhaps the first week I was in shiur, at the conclusion of a long series of medical prescriptions, many of which seem quite at odds with our current medical knowledge and practices: "Congratulations, you're all EMTs now."

Yet at the beginning of the following week, Asher summarized the lesson from that same day's shiur—"Rabbi Nassan was a dayan, and he descends to the profundities of the law"—as: we don't understand it "but he was a dayan" and we just have to accept [his ruling]. And in shiur the same day, the Rosh Yeshiva confirmed this understanding:

"We don't understand Rabbi Nassan's reasoning, 'but he's a dayan' so we follow him."

What should we make of what appear to be two contradictory principles? The first is that authority should be accepted even if we don't understand it, and the other that we cannot act according to the views of an authority whom we do not understand. Perhaps, one lesson is that bits of the Talmud should not be extracted as decontextualized wisdom (or, God forbid, as decontextualized foolishness) but rather that most of this ultimately makes most sense in its own context—which I struggle and, as is inevitable in ethnography, fail adequately to provide here.

Taking Tosafos Seriously

One day early in my kollel year I was away from the yeshiva, out of town at a gathering of historians of early modern Jewish culture and society. I told one of them, a senior professor who had himself gone to yeshiva in his youth, about my studies in the yeshiva. What he most wanted to know was whether I saw any signs of genuine intellectual ambition, which he felt had been lost between the generation of older yeshiva scholars he knew as a youngster and the younger teachers he had even then. "Do they really try to understand and wrestle with Tosafos?" seemed to be one of his key criteria for sensing whether that courageous intellectual engagement is still found anywhere. "Or do they just recite the text with Rashi and Tosafos, and move on?"

In shiur later that same week, after we'd been through the text and Rashi, the Rosh Yeshiva said: "Okay, now we come to a Tosafos that . . . I don't know how to work it." The issue (already mentioned in the previous chapter) is a hypothetical case where a husband declares, "You are hereby divorced from me on condition you marry X." The rabbis of the Talmud don't like the idea of her doing so, because it might sound like a "gift" of a wife from one man to another. They accordingly pronounce the condition void if she attempts to carry it out directly. However, they suggest that she might marry another man, then validate the divorce by marrying X, thus performing the condition of the divorce: no one would say that this was a "gift" of a wife, since in the meantime she was with a stranger. Then, by marrying X, she would become fully a divorcée, and thereby validate her marriage to the stranger. . . . There, of course, is the rub, as the Rosh Yeshiva insisted repeatedly in trying to understand Tosafos's comment on this complex set of transactions: when she marries X she now, at the same time, becomes married to the stranger—and she obviously can't be married to two men!

"It's a recurring loop, as we call it in computer programming," Pinsker murmured to me.

At one point, the Rosh Yeshiva suggested that our problem "getting" the Tosafos might be more simple: "It's possible that if Tosafos was here and spoke our language, we wouldn't have this problem."

Taking the Torah Seriously

In chapter 3 I discussed the passage in tractate Sotah that explains that King David was punished for describing Torah as *zemiros*, or "melodies." The Rebbi explained this by contrasting it to the very careful language that some Jews use when referring to Rashi: "It's like the real *frummies* [pious ones] say, *der hayliker Rashi* [the holy Rashi]." He pronounced the word *haylik* with the vowel "ay" (as in "mine"), characteristic of the Yiddish of most regions where Hasidism predominated, instead of the "ey" vowel (as in "take"), which he would have learned from his own father and the Lithuanian yeshiva milieu, thus suggesting that the "real frummies" are likely to be Hasidim. I took the meaning of his analogy to be this: just as David, in the estimation of the Gemara, was overly familiar with the Torah, the intention of the "real frummies" here is not to pretend to be too familiar with Rashi, not to pretend we're his equals. Moreover, their intention is praiseworthy even if it tends to take the form of what seems to us overexaggerated piety. Indeed, the Rosh Yeshiva added: "Really, we should say *der hayliker mishne toyre*," referring to the title of Maimonides's monumental code of Jewish law.

The Rebbi, I suggested afterward to Asher, is trying to strike a balance here. On the one hand, we should try to understand the point of rebuking someone at the level of King David for not having taken the Torah more solemnly. On the other hand, we shouldn't pretend that we're at that level when we're not.

Asher picked up on the notion of someone pretentiously "learning a lesson" from the rebuke of King David: "You should learn with a *nigun* [melody] of Lamentations, not with a nigun of the Song of Songs."

Later, I joked with Rabbi Weiss that I'll be careful not to say I'm enjoying Torah too much, not to compare it to zemiros.

"You don't have to worry," he replied, reminding me that I'm not at the level where I'd be rebuked for enjoying it too much.

According to the Suffering Is the Reward

The Gemara at Bava Kama 38a discusses whether Gentiles, who are not obligated to observe the vast majority of the commandments in the Torah, are nevertheless rewarded if they do observe those commandments. It concludes that they are indeed rewarded, but less than Jews—because "one who is commanded and does is superior to one who is not commanded and does." The Rebbi explained that this is because of the anxiety attendant upon the obligation in anticipation: "Why does the one who is commanded get a greater reward? Because the thought, 'I must do it,' is weighing on my mind long before the obligation actually comes into force." He reinforced this argument with the maxim *lepum tsaarah skharah*, "according to the suffering is the reward."

Yisroel Ruven protested that this is unfair: if the suffering involved is the measure of the reward, then a Gentile who suffers for the sake of observing a commandment should be rewarded, even if he is not obligated.

The Rebbi responded by pointing to the analogous case of a Jewish woman who is not obligated to do a certain mitzvah, but does it anyway. He stated that "according to the suffering is the reward" applies to her, and concluded that perhaps indeed it should apply to a Gentile as well. This led to a brief mention of women who insist on putting on tefillin, against the usual Orthodox practice and sometimes in the face of mockery and protest.

The Rebbi remarked: "Those people [women] who [put on tefil-lin] must be getting lots of reward, because look at all the grief they're getting!"

Yet he was still troubled by Yisroel Ruven's question: it's still hard to understand why a Gentile is not rewarded according to his suffering. He suggested that perhaps God makes sure that righteous Gentiles who want to observe commandments don't suffer for it, and thus they miss out on the corresponding rewards. And he conceded that perhaps those truly compulsive Gentiles who not only observe the commandments, but worry about them beforehand, are in fact rewarded commensurately.

"Yeah," Yisroel Ruven commented when I reviewed this discussion with him after the shiur, "but he also said God wants it that way [with greater rewards for those who are commanded than for those who are not], so we'll have to work it out ourselves."

The Manor to Which He Has Become Accustomed

The Gemara at Bava Kama 7a notes that someone who owns houses is not obligated to sell them in order to provide food for himself. Instead, he can sustain himself by partaking of the tithes that are designated for the poor. Someone asked whether a person can be forced to sell a million-dollar house and move into a half-million-dollar house, rather than accept charity. This reminded the Rebbi of a joke about the practice, occasionally observed in synagogues, of subdividing portions of the Torah reading so that more than the prescribed number of congregants can be called up to recite the appropriate blessings. The extra aliyah (summons to recite the blessing over a section of the Torah reading) is called a hasofah (addition). "A man is given an aliyah. He comes up to the bimah and recites the blessing, 'Who created all things' [an all-purpose blessing, rather than the blessing specific to recitation from the Torah reading]. They ask him why, and he says, 'Well, I didn't know what blessing you're supposed to recite on a hasofah, so I made the blessing that covers everything.'" (As if to say, "Why didn't you give me a full aliyah, rather than just an extra one you carved out?")

"It's the same thing here: 'You call this living' [in the half-million-dollar house]?"

The implication might be that, indeed, no one can be forced to lower the quality of his dwelling in order to provide even for his own food. However, we also know that one who gets an additional aliyah should in fact recite the same blessing as everyone else who is called to the Torah. Thus, by analogy to that known rule, the rule here might be that a half-million-dollar house is just as much a dwelling as a million-dollar house, so one would indeed be obligated to "downsize" in order to provide himself with food from his own funds. Characteristically, the Rebbi refused to offer on the spot a clear ruling on a matter that's entirely hypothetical.

The Sotah Guy

Much of the tractate Sotah deals with its ostensible topic, the procedure for testing the loyalty of a woman whose husband suspects her of infidelity. As the Bible describes the situation, the entire process is initiated when a man warns his wife not to seclude herself with another man. Once he has done so, her seclusion with another man, as attested by valid witnesses, culminates in the ceremony of her drinking bitter waters and waiting to see whether her stomach swells and bursts (in which case she is deemed guilty) or nothing happens (in which case she may return to her husband). The question arises: May the man accomplish the initial warning on his own testimony (that is, without two additional witnesses to the warning), and even only by having suspicious thoughts about her? The Gemara leaves the matter in suspense. Therefore, one of the rabbis in the text notes: In case this view is right, then today (when there is no Temple, and therefore the ritual of the waters cannot be carried out, even where it is mandated as a result of the events just mentioned), a man should be very careful not to suspect his wife. If he does, and there is testimony to the wife's subsequent seclusion with the other man, he will not be allowed to remain with her and she will have no chance to prove her innocence through the ritual so that they may be reunited. However (still, on the hypothetical that such mental suspicions are effective to start the process), if he forgives his wife before the seclusion with the second man, then the ritual process would not have been initiated in any case. Asher told me, "There was a guy who used to call the Rosh Yeshiva and say, 'I think I suspected my wife. What should I do?' And the Rosh Yeshiva would say each time, 'Forgive her . . . Forgive her.' The [Rosh Yeshiva's] kids would pick up the phone, hear who it was, and say, '*Tati* [Dad], it's the sotah guy.' One time the caller said to the Rosh Yeshiva, 'You should know I'm a Talmud teacher, I'm not just a crazy guy.' [But the Rosh Yeshiva concluded,] One thing has nothing to do with the other."

Mirror Image

Nasanel says that when he looks at our teacher, he sees two people: one is the Rosh Yeshiva, who has an official role and must be careful with what he says. The other is known by his first name, is actually quite radical, and will, at times, if you're paying close attention, share some of those radical thoughts. "Sometimes he gives me this look, and we look at each other, both parts looking at the other's opposite part. The Rosh Yeshiva looks at the rebel [in me, Nasanel] and I look at———," each facet of each one's personality challenging the other.

I also know that look of the Rebbi's, and though it's tempting for the sake of the ethnography to imagine that he's looking at both the skeptical ethnographer and the yearning Talmud student, I don't actually presume to know what he's thinking. I've gotten the look a few times now, sometimes in the beis medresh on long Shabbes afternoons in the summer. He looks at me, I smile trying to look respectful, friendly, and not stupid all at once, and I find I am struck quite mute.

Study Leads to Action

The end of the first chapter of Bava Kama (17a) deals with the question of the relative priorities of Torah study versus the active performance of commandments. The Rosh Yeshiva explained more subtly the meaning of the dictum that study is great because it leads to the performance of mitzvos. It's not because when I study, I know how to do mitzvos; on the contrary, "The more I learn, the more I'm *fartift* [engrossed], the more I know I don't know." This will make me stand in greater awe of Heaven, and thus encourage me to follow the commandments more diligently.

How Rebbi Learns

One day Asher, Hillel, and I understood the Gemara (at the bottom of Bava Kama 21b) the same way the Rebbi understood it in shiur, and our agreement that Tosafos's explanation of the scenario the Gemara was discussing seemed to make the most sense was evidently in accord with the Rosh Yeshiva's reading as well. I pointed this out to Asher, who replied, "Yeah, wasn't that satisfying? Every now and then I see that I'm reading the Gemara the way the Rosh Yeshiva learns it. Somebody asked me once years ago why I go to the shiur, and I said it's because I hope that if I stay long enough, sometimes I'll learn the way he does. I'll never really get there, but every year I get a little closer to how the Rebbi learns."

100 Times, Then 101

Reviewing today's Gemara with Asher, I remark, "I've got the analytic skills, but I have a lousy memory."

Asher: "It's like the Rosh Yeshiva says: You gotta learn it like a broken record. Learn it a hundred times, then learn it again."

5

The Meaning of *Leshma*

FOR A FEW YEARS in the mid-1980s I was part of an adult beginners' study group that met in the beis medresh of MTJ. Two young rabbis, one a Hasid from Brooklyn and the other a streetwise native Lower East Sider, were our teachers. Years after I stopped participating in that group, our teacher from the East Side was honored by a Brooklyn yeshiva. I took out a full-page ad in the dinner journal that read, "Thank you,——, for teaching me the meaning of *leshma*."

My former teacher knew what I meant by that word: roughly, doing something good for its own sake, rather than with an ulterior motive. But with amusement, he reported to me later, "Everybody asked, what does that mean? Did Jonathan mean, [the study of] Torah leshma?"

The story has stuck with me for decades, in part because I do believe that I saw my teacher giving us his time and care *leshma*, yet—despite what I wrote—I've never been sure I'd be able to explain to someone else exactly what the word means. During my time at the yeshiva, the term has thus become a way to gather together and reflect on a range of moments that reflect the productive and agonizing tension between goal-oriented behavior and actions that are devoted to their own moment.

The focus on leshma was fostered by a passage of Talmud I happened to encounter just a couple of weeks into my kollel year, on

December 24, 2011. For years, on and off, I'd been carrying on my personal daf yomi discipline, studying a folio of Babylonian Talmud every day, although not on the same schedule as those involved in the worldwide study movement that goes under that name. For the previous few months, in fact, I'd been doubling up and covering two folios per day, since the Stanton Street Shul's centennial year was coming up in 2013, and I'd realized that completion of the entire Talmud was in reach for me sometime during that year. This is a much more superficial form of study than a class such as the Rosh Yeshiva's—or at least it's easier for someone such as myself, who isn't really experienced at reading the text of the Talmud and commentaries on my own and in the original language. Every now and then a passage strikes me as particularly noteworthy, and I flag it with a Post-it note at the margins. (I even wrote a paper called "Post-It Notes of an ArtScroll Amateur.")[1] More occasionally, I happen to come across a text in the course of my self-study that helps me address something that's pertinent to what I'm working on or wondering about at that moment. What had challenged me that Saturday morning, and kept me from concentrating on prayer, was the question of how to imagine a book based on a year at the yeshiva. The question was hugely premature, since I didn't really know what the year might bring. It was also timely, since my experiences are shaped very much by my writing. Moreover, worrying about how to write about Torah study seemed to present something of a moral challenge, since the ideal is indeed *Torah leshma*—the study of Torah for its own sake, and certainly not for professional advancement in the secular world.

This was the talmudic text that came to offer a bit of guidance, found in the tractate Sukkah at folio 49b, which I quote in ArtScroll's translation and "elucidation." Having presented a number of dicta, not necessarily related by theme but all attributed to Rabbi Elazar, the series concludes with this:

> And R' Elazar said: What is meant by that which is written: "*She opens her mouth with wisdom and the Torah of kindness is upon*

her tongue?" Now, is there a Torah of kindness and a Torah that is not of kindness? Rather, the implied distinction is this: Torah that is studied for its own sake is referred to as a Torah of kindness [and Torah] not for its own sake is considered a Torah that is not of kindness.

There are those who say that the distinction was stated as follows: Torah that is studied with the intention of teaching it to others is referred to as a Torah of kindness. However, Torah that is studied without the intention of teaching it to others is considered a Torah that is not of kindness.

The rabbis do not, in this case, determine which interpretation is correct, perhaps because they did not necessarily see any practical difference between them. That is, within the scheme of filiation and transmission of Torah as they understood it, learning in order to convey the tradition in turn *is* learning for its own sake. Yet it struck me that in my situation, there was a difference. According to the first version of Rabbi Elazar's distinction, if I have an ulterior motive in my study (in this case, to gain inspiration or subject matter for my writing), then I am not practicing the best form of Torah. Yet according to the second version, if I see my writing as a form of teaching, I am indeed practicing the Torah of kindness.

Those wiser than I would likely advise me not to worry too much about whether my study is leshma. This is true not only because, as Rav Yehudah, quoting Rav, says "A person should always occupy himself in Torah and in mitzvos even not for its own sake," because eventually he will come to do it for its own sake (Arachin 16b). Indeed, at least some acquaintances at the beis medresh knew when I came there that I was an academic chronicler of life on the Lower East Side.

There is, nonetheless, a real tension, under either version of Rabbi Elazar's definition of "the Torah of kindness." According to the first version, ultimately the writing, too, should be for its own sake, or the precious coincidence of time and consciousness that we sometimes call true presence is lost. According to the second version, ultimately as well, the writing must at least strive to be a form of teaching.

As I struggled with this tension, I came up with a formula in an attempt to resolve my dilemma about whether to describe my time at MTJ as for its own sake or not (that is, in a nutshell, whether to sell myself short or to oversell myself). It's true that, as a tenured full professor, I am in a privileged enough situation at the moment to say that I would indeed have spent that year at MTJ even if I had no writerly ambitions with regard to the experience. Nevertheless, writing does help me give the experience shape and helps me fit it into my own life. The desire to live this life comes first if anything comes first, but the reflection and recording are not merely ancillary. Decades ago, in my first publication about the Jewish community of the Lower East Side, I had coined (I think) the phrase "observant participation,"[2] a bit of a pun on the notion of an "observant" Jew. Here I am trying out the concept of *mitokh leshma yavo shelo leshma*: out of what is done for its own sake (the study) can come that which is not for its own sake (the ethnography). Not what Rav Yehudah had in mind, of course, but not necessarily a bad thing either.

I tried out that phrase on an acquaintance at the Bialystoker Shul, a history teacher at the Modern Orthodox Ramaz School on the Upper East Side who is also a former humor editor of *Heeb* magazine, which was altogether irreverent and aimed at "hip" young Jewish adults. This teacher completed all but a dissertation in Jewish history himself, and has a brother who teaches Jewish studies at the University of California, Santa Cruz. He suggested that I shouldn't worry so much about trying to write for an academic audience and for those in the beis medresh at the same time: "But you've really got a free pass, because whatever you write about the yeshiva, they won't read it anyway." Yet that isn't necessarily so, as evidenced, for example, by one MTJ regular's reference in conversation with me to William Helmreich's *The World of the Yeshiva*.

The notion of leshma—in the "larger" sense of studying or doing anything for its own sake, and not as a means to an end—also echoes the threatened and perhaps vanishing understanding of a "liberal education" as worthwhile in its own right. Similar to the word "modern," the word "liberal" means many different things. Thus, it happens that one way to describe the attack on liberal education is to identify that attack with what is called "neoliberalism," the revival of older ideas of free-market, laissez-faire capitalism and its spread to new aspects of life, linked in turn to the diminution of scope of the welfare state. I was inspired to think of old-fashioned liberal education (with all its elitism and rigidity) in the framework of leshma by a talk the Berkeley political theorist Wendy Brown gave at Cornell in the fall of 2013, titled "The Demos Undone: Neoliberalism, Democracy, Citizenship." The website blurb for the talk read:

> Neoliberalism is more than a set of economic policies. As a form of reason developed into a governing rationality, it converts every aspect of contemporary existence into a market framework. All conduct is market conduct, all spheres of existence are market-like. This lecture will address the dismantling of democratic imaginaries and democratic practices by this rationality.

Upon hearing the title of the talk, my reaction was "but we knew that already." And yet in the days after Brown's talk, I was more and more convinced by her account of a progressive spread of capitalist thinking (what she calls "capitalization," although that may be a somewhat idiosyncratic use of the term) into the university, electoral politics, and the like, and the concomitant diminution of a notion of civics.

This led me to think of the yeshiva as a space where, with all due caveats about ethnographic sentimentalism firmly in place, neoliberal rationality does not hold sway. That is: the participants in the beis medresh are not profit-maximizing, rational individual actors, neither in their behavior nor (as I infer from my interactions with them) in their consciousness. Although ideologies of collecting mitzvos for the World to Come (and even of helping to bring Messiah to this world) are available, they are not primarily what drives attendance at the yeshiva. Rather, the driving force is the sense that this is what a male Jew should be doing—even though it's clearly acknowledged that there are other valid pressures, that sometimes, as the Rosh Yeshiva said to me, "You gotta work." But neither the rhetoric nor the casual conversation before the shiur suggests that anyone is just marking time at the yeshiva. Rather, the goal seems to be the unmarking of time. As my brother Daniel wrote long ago in *The Second Jewish Catalogue*: "Time stops in the world of Talmud Torah. A question asked in the sixteenth century is answered in the eleventh."

I would say today—no, time does not stop in the world of the beis medresh; but its vectors are multiple. Later commentators may certainly illuminate earlier texts, and in that sense there is "progress" of a sort. Yet there is a haunting sense, continuing from the Gemara's attempt to harmonize the Mishnah on to group study today, that the commentaries are only necessary because of what has been lost—along with an underlying commitment to rereading the earlier texts on our own, as if for the first time, without (at least initially) being guided by those commentaries, and thus willfully ignoring or slowing down "progress." And certainly, there is no suggestion that our goal, individual or collective, is to achieve an overarching comprehension of the rabbinic canon that somehow escaped our predecessors.

Day to day, day after day, the imperative of "getting somewhere" is resisted at the tables of the beis medresh, partly because doing so would imply a claim of having mastered the texts that are then "left behind." Thus, there is a constant tug between reviewing and studying new material. This was clearly observed, and expressed back to me, by the same Israeli guest who had sat in on the shiur when the Rosh Yeshiva commented on the Gemara's assertion that "Rabbi Nassan was a dayan." At my suggestion, he met me at my apartment and we walked down Essex Street to the yeshiva together. On the way I tried to explain to him some of the ideas I was trying out as themes for an ethnography, but didn't manage to explain to him very well my idea about the special temporality of the yeshiva. After shiur, as we walked back uptown, he understood it very well. "So they [e.g., Asher and Hillel] study the same thing three times," he observed. I told him that's correct—preparing for shiur, in shiur, and reviewing after shiur.

It's not about producing anything, I said, as I've said to many others.

"Right, it's about the time you spend doing it," he responded. It recalled to him his time in Tibet: "The monks there spend a month preparing sand mandalas for the festival of the birthday of the Buddha, and then they spend a month contemplating them, and then they brush them away. And I was there taking pictures of them with my camera."

Some Meanings of Leshma

So time has something to do with leshma, and noninstrumentality has something to do with it—but isn't that just another way of saying "for its own sake"? I'm still troubled by the implicit claim I made in that dedication to my teacher about "the meaning of leshma." He had taught me something important, yet it's something that I still can't quite articulate. The best I can do, perhaps, is to share a set of anecdotes and musings that the word continues to evoke, and perhaps that will serve better than any definition could.

The More Leshma, the Less Ethnography?

Early on in my kollel year I found that the more I got into study leshma the harder it was to keep good notes. This wasn't because the goals of participating and recording are necessarily at cross-purposes. I'm not convinced they are, and as mentioned earlier, someone writing notes in the beis medresh is hardly unusual or conspicuous. Rather, being fully engaged in a group study session means not taking time out to keep good notes. It's more like trying to drive and text at the same time than it is like being two persons inside one brain, one "religious" and one "secular."

That's true even when I'm only able to make a brief appearance at the yeshiva on a short break from my university schedule. At the end of my first semester at Cornell, I got back to the East Side from Ithaca around 3:30 p.m. Elissa was out, so I grabbed the opportunity to spend a couple of hours with Asher and then with Hillel as they prepared for the next day's shiur, which I missed as Elissa and I were heading to the American Anthropological Association meetings in Washington, DC. During those precious hours, I failed to take any notes and chalked it up as one of my "undoing ethnography" days. Yet a story Asher told me while I was there stayed in my mind, so I wrote it down after I'd gotten home.

When I came in, he was sitting by himself, looking at some of the commentators in the back of a volume of Talmud. I mentioned to him Abraham Joshua Heschel's citation, in his Yiddish book about the Rebbe of Kotsk, of the saying that when one studies the text of a commentator, he should read it as though it were a letter from one's father. Asher liked that, and in response, said to me, "You know, my grandfather was a teacher in the high school at Yeshiva University, so he got to know Reb Dov Ber Soloveitchik [the revered rosh yeshiva there]. One day my grandfather said to him, 'The Rebbi is a great *masmid* [diligent scholar].'"

"Rabbi Soloveitchik said to him, 'Not as much as I used to be. When I was young I lived with the Rishonim day and night. I'd wake up with them and go to sleep with them. When I had to go to sleep, it made me sad to say goodbye to them.'"

If my study was completely leshma and I wasn't doing ethnography, would I have remembered this story?

Leshma and Leshem shamayim

Obviously linked to leshma linguistically, but not very often in conversation, is the notion of *leshem shamayim*, doing something "for the sake of heaven." Both terms entail the absence of ulterior motive. Perhaps they differ most in that leshma standing alone focuses on the value of the activity in its own right, while leshem shamayim has more to do with the purity of the actor's motives.

The latter term came up one morning before shiur. We started talking about Rabbi Joseph Singer, my rabbi at the Stanton Street Shul until the year 2000. I wanted to get in a funny story having to do with the near homonym of the English word "roof" with the word *ruv* (Yiddish for "rabbi," according to the pronunciation of the province of Galicia). Once I mentioned Rabbi Singer, Yisroel Ruven started reminiscing what a tzaddik he had been. I said, "He was my rabbi—that's why I'm involved with that shul," seeing a chance to shore up my legitimacy despite the fact that Stanton Street is now a more "modern" Orthodox congregation whose rabbi does not accede to the authority of the Rosh Yeshiva on all issues.

Yisroel Ruven understood that point very well, and replied that Rabbi Singer wouldn't approve of the Stanton Street Shul now: "He was fully traditional. Everything he did was leshem shamayim. I'm a friend of his cousin Mendl Farber from the Bialystoker Shul. Back in the '70s, Mendl was a slumlord. There used to be a park right near that shul, on the way from the co-ops."

"Yeah," I said, "the schoolyard on Attorney Street, between Stanton and Rivington."

Yisroel Ruven continued, "It was full of crackheads, and he would walk through there. Some of Mendl's workers knew the junkies, and they said, 'If anybody touches the rabbi, we'll kill him.'" The suggestion here is that Rabbi Singer was so holy that even the junkies recognized that quality in him. I have no doubt this is correct.

If You Don't Understand It, Is It Leshma?

In my solo study, I certainly do set "production" goals for myself: a folio a day of the ArtScroll Talmud, or, while I was working through the volume of the *Tur* on marriage and family law, together with *Beis Yosef*'s commentary—two pages a day until I finished, at a date projected several months beforehand. That study was clearly goal oriented; I sought the Rosh Yeshiva's approbation, and was motivated in part by his telling me "you should finish the book," when I had made a ceremony out of completing only one small section of it. On the other hand, what could be more "for its own sake?" I'm far from understanding everything I read in that book, so in a sense, even if I had an ulterior motive it would be hard to see what I could accomplish. Moreover, if I wanted to know the law in practice, I would go straight to the successor compendium known as the *Shulchan aruch*, regarded as the baseline halachic authority for Orthodox Jews from its first publication in the sixteenth century until today.

Leshma and Payment

Very near the beginning of the tractate in Mishnah known as Ethics of the Fathers we read the statement of Antigonos of Socho: "Do not be as slaves, who serve their master for the sake of reward. Rather, be as slaves who serve their master not for the sake of reward." But what if this ethnography were the "payment" for my time at the yeshiva—in two senses of the term, that is, the recompense that is owing to me, and the product that I owe to the academy that supports me? If I truly were intent on proving that my own study was leshma, that might dictate that I fail to present this book, both to my colleagues at the university and to my friends at the yeshiva. And yet here it is.

Leshma and the Enduring Record

Every year I dutifully attend the annual dinner that benefits both the kollel of MTJ and that of its sister yeshiva (run by our Rosh Yeshiva's brother) in Staten Island. The fried chicken at the cocktail-hour buffet is the best part. The sit-down dinner and speeches, not so much. Elissa does not join me, because although women do attend, they are separated from the larger area where men sit by a high barrier that makes the speakers invisible to them.

At the dinner in May 2015, a young man (evidently a rabbi according to the seating chart, although he didn't use the title when he introduced himself) sat down next to me. He's a social worker who works with Shlomo Farber, another alumnus of the Rosh Yeshiva's shiur, in a federally funded school tutoring program. When I mentioned that I'm an anthropologist and I wrote a book about my shul, he asked my name and got excited: "You wrote the book about the Stanton Street Shul! I loved the story about the man in the daily minyan who used to say in Hebrew, 'today is every day' instead of 'today is the *n*th day of the week.'" Later he said to me, "I'm jealous of you, but it's okay because it's *kinas sofrim* [literary envy]. You get to write things that are *lanetsakh* [a permanent record, as opposed to ephemera]." This suggests that, at least in some corners of the yeshiva world, the opportunity to do the kind of academic writing I'm committed to is seen as a privilege, rather than a distraction.

Can Leshma Be a Form of Censorship?

During my kollel year, I found myself the confidant of a young man who was clearly ready to move on from the beis medresh, which he found somewhat intellectually confining. One day we were discussing the ArtScroll Talmud. I frequently see it being used in the beis medresh, yet it is regarded with a certain degree of ambivalence, as a kind of cheat sheet, a shortcut to what should be arduous study. My friend criticized this attitude: "The Soncino [an older translation into English] and ArtScroll aren't [considered] kosher. . . . Well, it depends what your goal is. Do you want to *know* it [academically] or do you want to *learn* it? To know it, you have to use any means possible." Though I did not draw him out further, I think his suggestion here was that if a tool is available, it should be used, and that to insist only on older and slower means of study is to indulge in a kind of mystification for which, perhaps, the ideal of leshma might serve as a vehicle. And although he expressed impatience with those who may not be primarily interested in "knowing" it, his comment also implicitly recognized that "learning" might also be a goal in itself.

To be sure, some of the rabbis of the Talmud might have taken umbrage at my half-serious suggestion above that I can tell I'm studying leshma because I don't remember most of what I'm studying. Yet certainly they were concerned with questions of memory and forgetting:

> Ulla said: "Thoughts [Rashi says: 'worries about sustenance'] cause one to forget Torah." Rabbah said: "Those who are engaged in Torah study leshma will not forget as a result of such worry . . . [for] counsel that contains the word of God will last forever." (Sanhedrin 26b)

Nasanel, too, counseled me that "just doing it" in the moment, without any concern for the accumulation of knowledge, isn't sufficient. One day when I was quite content to spend almost an hour in philosophical conversation with him, I asked him whether Torah can be a contemplative practice. He answers: "I addressed that question already. I told you that. Subconsciously you remember. The Vilna Gaon said that if all was required was *yegiya batoyre* [effort in Torah], he could have spent his entire life on the first folio of Bava Metsiya. But we need to have *yediyas hatoyre* [knowledge of the Torah] as well."

Future Reward

I don't know how much the expectation of reward in the World to Come motivates my comrades at the yeshiva. As I've mentioned, it's not talked about very much. Yet when it does enter the conversation, it seems entirely normative, rather than pietistic or overly credulous.

Before I departed one afternoon, Rabbi Cantor asked for a few minutes of my time. He had given me a blessing the day before, and he repeated it, while holding my right hand in both of his: I and my entire family should have *nachas* (emotional satisfaction) and I should, so to speak, give nachas to God as well. He had two specific recommendations to help me realize that blessing. First, in addition to having a set time for my studies, I should make sure to spend some time studying both during the daylight hours and at night, as the Torah says, "You shall meditate on it day and night" (Joshua 1:6). Second, he told me I should study at least two *hala-chos* (points of applied Jewish law) a day, as the rabbis say: "Who-ever studies halachos [the term is plural, hence requiring at least two] every day is assured of being a 'son of the World to Come.'"

Enough Already with Leshma

This question has, I think, been productive for trying to under-stand not so much the morality, but the temporality of the beis medresh. It seriously troubled me for a few months, but at some point I decided I was finished, at least for the time being, with the attempt to decide whether my time at the yeshiva was being spent leshma or not. Who needs an excuse one way or the other? said I to myself. Part of the reason I decided to let it go was that I found out why Simcha Goldman, in his study sessions with me, had de-cided he wanted to study the passage of the *Tur* dealing with the hypothetical applicability in the present of the biblical law requir-ing cancellation of debts in the sabbatical year. He was writing an article about it.

6

The Professor

ANTHROPOLOGISTS ARE USED to being awkward beginners. Sometimes it's because we're engaging in the classic method of participant observation, trying to find the rhythm of a dance we didn't grow up doing, and avoid confusing those in front of and behind us at the same time. Sometimes it's because anthropology isn't the smoothest career path these days, and we have to find something else to do for a living, temporarily or permanently. I found myself in the latter situation at the end of the 1990s, as a junior associate at a major New York corporate law firm. I was in my early forties, and thus as old as or even older than many of the partners under whom I was working. The gap was, if anything, intensified by my working in the tax department—a field where almost nothing is intuitive and very little can be accomplished by those without long years of specialized experience. In retrospect, it was an extraordinary experience, but at the time I was plagued by a vacillation between two equally unproductive reactions: "I'm as old as she is, how can it be that she knows everything and I know nothing?" and "I'm as old as she is, how come she makes ten times as much money as I do?"

If I vacillated in my evaluation of myself vis-à-vis more experienced others at the yeshiva, the stakes were certainly different. For one thing, money had nothing to do with it. More pertinent were my concerns about whether I was capable of learning with the big boys, and whether the academic learning (and scattered experiences of Talmud study) that I brought with me would translate into intellectual currency at MTJ.

To be sure, no one ever questioned my right to sit and study at MTJ, and I never once heard a hint that I wasn't quite ready. But on the question of the value of my secular scholarship—or at least, its relevance to Torah—there may have been some doubts. As mentioned above, I spent several months studying the Mishnah with Petrushka's Yiddish commentary with Nasanel. Nasanel had decided we should focus on the tractate Kilaim, a rarely studied text that deals with the rules about forbidden mixtures of planted crops. He also decided that we should go back to the beginning of the entire mishnaic corpus and study Petrushka on the tractate Berachos (blessings), with the goal of eventually studying together all of the Mishnah.

Mishnah Berachos 4:3 reads: "Rabbi Nechunya ben Hakana used to pray a short prayer upon entering and upon leaving the beis medresh. They asked him, 'How is this a place of prayer?' He said to them, 'When I go in I pray that no harm may come through me, and when I leave I give thanks for my share [in Torah].'" I asked Nasanel whether I should recite this prayer when I go to my office at the university. He said yes, what I do there is holy work. He cited as authority the tradition of Torah study associated with the city of Brisk and the family Soloveitchik. According to Nasanel, in the tradition of Brisk they say that everything is Torah, the whole world is Torah. But when I asked another acquaintance who happened to be standing nearby the same question, he asked rather skeptically, "This [what you teach at the university] is Torah???" So apparently for him there are some things that are Torah, and some things that just aren't.

Another source of self-doubt is my sense, already mentioned, that my retention is poor. To be sure, everyone knows that what one learns younger stays with one longer, and the rabbis knew it as well. In a famous mishnaic dictum, Elisha b. Avuya says, "One who learns when young, to what may he be compared? To ink written on fresh paper. But one who learns when old, to what may he be compared? To ink written on paper that has been erased" (Avot 4:20). Beyond the fact that I'm coming late to the table, I've long thought of myself as one who's better at asking unexpected questions than at retaining details of texts or logical patterns in my head. Given these doubts, I tried to attend particularly closely to a mussar shmues of the Mashgiach's in the late fall of 2012 that seemed to bear on the question of retention.

He spoke about the way Hurricane Sandy had broken many trees: "I understand [it came in the autumn], they were heavy with leaves, they didn't have sap, so they were brittle and vulnerable to the wind, there's a good natural explanation for that," but how could it have uprooted so many trees altogether? He was drawing on this dramatic recent event to illustrate the teaching of the Mishnah in Ethics of the Fathers 3:17, which reads:

> Rabbi Eleazar ben Azariah said: . . . One whose wisdom exceeds his deeds, unto what is he compared? Unto a tree the branches whereof are many and the roots few, so that when the wind comes, it uproots it and overturns it upon its face. . . . But one whose deeds exceed his wisdom, unto what is he compared? Unto a tree the branches whereof are few and the roots many, so that even if all the winds in the world come and blow upon it, they move it not out of its place.

He further related this notion of—shall we say—*groundedness* to another mishnah in the same chapter (3:9): "Rabbi Chanina b. Dosa said: 'Anyone whose fear of sin precedes his wisdom, his wisdom is enduring, but anyone whose wisdom precedes his fear of sin, his wisdom is not enduring.'"

After the Mashgiach finished, I approached him to ask about the meaning of the Hebrew words translated as "his wisdom is enduring." Do they mean that he will remember what he learns, or that his learning will stand by him [in the World to Come]? He replied, "It means that it becomes integrated, it becomes part of you."

Where I stand vis-à-vis either of these mishnayos, I don't know. Yet I have received perhaps more than my due share of encouragement from my fellows at MTJ. Right after New Year's Day 2012, thus, early in my kollel year, I entered the beis medresh somewhat dopey with a head cold, only slightly relieved by Sudafed. We were working on a Gemara in tractate Gittin that was devoted to an attempted reconciliation of two parts of a single mishnah so that they could both be credited to the same Tanna, either Rabbi Meir or Rabbi Yose. The issue at hand concerned the putative validity of person A making person B his agent to convey mere words of instruction, rather than his agent to carry out a physical act. It seemed to me I didn't follow even the preparation session very well, let alone the shiur itself. Nevertheless, as I was leaving, Yisroel Ruven graciously said, "I enjoy your presence. You know what's going on. You add to the mix." That was certainly heartening.

The same day I had a brief conversation with Rabbi Weiss, after spending some time with him and Rabbi Karp the previous week studying *Mishnah berurah*. He said, "It's a shame you're not with us anymore," almost like a new and jealous friend. "You sound like you learned in yeshiva." I denied it—accurately enough, at least to the extent that I had never spent time in yeshiva in my childhood and adolescence. "You get a lot of the points what's going on."

Occasionally the approbation would come from outside the beis medresh, albeit still within the frame of the Orthodox community. On winter break from my first semester at Cornell in mid-December 2013, I spent a couple of hours in the morning studying the ArtScroll edition of Bava Kama by myself. Then, after a quick half hour studying the *Tur* with Nasanel, Elissa and I went to visit our disabled son Yeshaya in Brooklyn. Returning to the East Side, I parked the car at my lot on Essex Street, in between home and MTJ. I asked Elissa if I might go back to the yeshiva for a couple of hours. She agreed, adding that an Orthodox female friend of hers had told her that "for middle-aged guys, it's good to spend time at the yeshiva. They feel like they're getting to do something they didn't necessarily count on at this stage of life."

Merging and Popping

My field notes from the beginning of this "project," 12/25/2011, give the lie to my claim that I don't think of the yeshiva as a separate "world":

> Years ago I used to think of anthropology as bubble science. I was never able to describe very well what I meant by that phrase. Yet it contained some notion of all of us living within a certain set of bubbles—worlds we had made and had placed ourselves into, or worlds we were constrained by—and of anthropologists as studying the surface tensions or even trying to push at the surfaces of those bubbles as a way to understand them and ourselves better. And I recall an understanding of this particular yeshiva's bubble that I had gained decades ago, when I came as a young adult "beginner" in the mid-1980s. It is not an "outreach" yeshiva, where they're thrilled to have someone come in who doesn't look the same or have the same background as everyone else in the room, because that someone is raw material to work on and hence "grow" the in-group. I may look somewhat different (I don't wear a suit and a black hat to the yeshiva), but I'm not especially interesting. Nor is it an insular yeshiva, part of a sub-community trying to maintain tightly its own boundaries. Again, I may look a bit different, but I'm not a particular threat to anybody's identity or way of life. It's a neighborhood yeshiva, and though I've lived on the Lower East Side for nearly forty years, as far as most of the people in the yeshiva are concerned I may still be a newcomer.

So, if I use the language of bubbles, it's not to suggest that I'm in one and everyone else at the yeshiva is in another, with no points of contact or interpenetration. On the contrary, perhaps one of the reasons why I consistently doubted whether I was really doing fieldwork at all is that the entry was, if anything, too easy and too warm. Fieldwork is supposed to present us with revealing boundaries, with the edges of bubbles, the places and pressures where they intersect, pop, stretch, combine.

One of my favorite personal examples of such a boundary literally happened at an intersection in my neighborhood. Many years ago, on a bitter winter day, I was walking past the corner of Eighth Street and Avenue A, across the street from Tompkins Square Park in the East Village, wearing a parka with a thick hood. I saw two teenage boys, recognizable by their dress as members of the Chabad hasidic group, standing on the corner. They looked like they might be lost, so I slowed down to try to figure out whether they needed help. Only later did I realize they were probably just looking for Jews whom they could induce to perform one of the 613 commandments. Perhaps because I hesitated as I passed by them, they asked me if I was Jewish, and then whether I had put on tefillin that day. I told them I had, and this caught them completely off guard: *"You did?!?!"* Once they found that out they completely lost interest in me, but their first reaction was to be entirely nonplussed. In telling the story over the years, I've described their reaction as similar to someone who's getting ready to break down a door with his shoulder, and just when he's run right up to it, someone opens the door so that he loses his balance and falls to the ground. I implicitly tease these young men, when I tell this story, for not knowing how to deal with someone who's already doing the things they're trying to get Jews to do. What threw them off was the lack of an expected boundary: I was already like them, while they were prepared to work to make me so, strenuously if needed. I try to take wisdom from their evident confusion, and avoid trying to construe MTJ in ways that would make it as alien to this ethnographer as a proper field site "should."

Faith Binds Us?

One would, to be sure, conventionally describe most of the regulars at MTJ as "more religious" than I. But I join a growing chorus of anthropologists who insist that "religiosity" is not a quantum, such that a given individual stands at a fixed point on a continuum from most secular to most religious. Implicit in this assertion is that those who appear "most religious" are most likely neither dupes nor willfully believe "because it is absurd," but rather, they, too, participate in a range of discourses with varying rules of engagement, and to varying degrees, they do so consciously even if they never speak of that range.

I wondered about this one morning before shiur, while we were studying the passages in Sotah about the stories of conquest under Joshua, and the discussion around the table concerned how the bunch of grapes was carried by the spies: Were extra poles actually needed to bear this heavy fruit, were they utilized to prevent bruising along the way? . . . What I find very hard to imagine is that anyone or almost anyone in the shiur reads the concerns of the Gemara about the book of Joshua as literally as the discourse in the shiur would suggest. I'm not at all sure the medieval commentators, such as the Tosafists, who spent so much time addressing these logistical questions, did either. Whether others think about this problem (I suppose it could be labeled the problem of miraculous divine intervention) or are troubled by it I can't say. I'm not, so I don't see why they should be.

On the other hand, while I know what's going on in my own head (sort of), I don't know what my fellows are thinking, so why project rather than ask? Why, you might wonder, didn't I ever just ask one of those seated around the table whether he "really believed" in these giant bunches of grapes and the various attendant miracles the midrash describes? Was it just a reluctance to undertake the hard work of talking to people to find out what their own conceptions are?

The literary allusion I decided to draw on in my own defense is, perhaps, a more poetic way of saying that I want neither to appear nor to be ultimately the "outsider" ethnographer. Who is the wicked son in the Passover Haggadah? The one who asks, "What does all this mean *to you*?"—interpreted as "to you and not to him," as he thereby excludes himself. Elsewhere, however, precisely this question is considered meritorious, as if it should be read, "What does all this mean to you, and therefore to me?" There is a way to ask the question as a request for the sharing of wisdom gained. Alas, most often the ethnographic interview is not that way.

Despite my best efforts at discretion, I sometimes revealed myself at least potentially as that wicked son who sees all this Torah as something pertinent to another and not to himself. During the intermediate days of Sukkot in 2012—a time when yeshiva is not in session, unnecessary work is enjoined, and thus otherwise doubtfully appropriate although innocuous pastimes are in order—Nasanel, Henoch, and I went to a New York Philharmonic concert at Lincoln Center. As we waited for the concert to begin, I asked them whether they'd ever been there before. It was Nasanel's first time, but Henoch had been there once before. "But it was for a benefit for HASC," the Hebrew Academy for Special Children.

I said, "Yeah, so that was different, because you were here with your community."

Nasanel immediately picked up on the pronoun: "You [anthropologist] said, 'your community.' You see, you're saying it's his community but not your community." I immediately heard echoes of the Haggadah's "to you, and not to him—had he been there he would not have been redeemed." Had I been there, would I have been redeemed? Yet Nasanel is fascinated by my moves between the university and the yeshiva, has stated his admiration for it, and is generally restrained about suggesting that I should be more in one of them and less in the other.

He has, however, tried to get me to view Sunday, and not just the secular weekdays, as a day for the yeshiva. And why not, given the riches I consistently find there? It's strange to have reached the time of life when there's nothing I'm particularly looking forward to (and hence the passage of time is not a good in itself), and instead I'm more concerned with making each moment as rich as it can be. I had these thoughts two days after slipping on the ice on my way to the Bialystoker Shul, grateful that I didn't hurt myself more than I could have; two weeks after taking a break from the gym because of a groin strain that I worried might be a hernia (and that came from rashly trying to move a heavy bookcase in the beis medresh); four days after a day when I had to remain in Ithaca and wait for the snow to pass so I could return to my "real life" in New York; the evening after my second day back in the gym (and quite tired because of it); less than an hour after venturing out, on a winter's evening that was nevertheless hardly as bitter as many we've had this winter, to walk to Chinatown for takeout from one of the vegetarian restaurants there, observing the people, signs, and broken sidewalks along the way more intensely than I have for quite some time, and wondering how I could turn that intensity into the only kind of art I know, which is writing. And, for the third day in a row, experiencing the worrisome sensation of not being able to remember a good vocabulary word. Effusive. Dialysis. Anachronistic.

Sitting in the beis medresh doesn't require much athletic stamina, and it's hardly great physical exercise. But it does demand mental acuity, and if it's true that exercising your brain helps stave off dementia, I will be well advised to sit and learn as long as I can. Anyway, it takes at least a serious attempt to understand what's going on in the text to do this kind of fieldwork, because the books lie at the center of the yeshiva life.

What kind of fieldwork is it where you have to check a published, printed text—not your own earlier work, not even that of another ethnographer—to make sense of your own notes? I had the fleeting, wistful thought one day that a lot of this work would be easier if I had a real academic Talmud scholar with me in the beis medresh. That feeling reminded me of the forlorn wish I had, when I was doing fieldwork in Paris over thirty years ago, to have a historian with me to explain all the detailed references I wasn't quite catching when elderly secular Polish Jews told me about the twists and turns of their remarkable life stories.

Shiva, Yeshiva

Sometimes, the field comes to you.

My mother Alice died in California early Wednesday morning, January 18, 2012. I received the news by phone from my brother Daniel as I was preparing to head to the yeshiva. I woke Elissa, told her the news, and told her I was heading to the yeshiva. She tried to dissuade me, perhaps thinking I planned to go through my usual study routine. Instead, I was somehow compelled to walk down to the yeshiva to explain why I wouldn't be there for some days, and to check with Rabbi Karp on some of the laws pertaining both to the period before the funeral, and to the period of shiva.

From the time of hearing of the death until the funeral, I was barred from the observance of all positive commandments, such as the wearing of tefillin and, most pertinently here, the study of Torah—either because mourners are expected to be preoccupied with funeral preparations at that time (which was not the case for me), or as a sign of general respect for the deceased. The ban on Torah study continues in force throughout the shiva period. I was thus required to be absent from the yeshiva, and sitting at home on the floor or on low benches, from Wednesday morning when I heard about the death, until the following Thursday morning, when the shiva period ended—though I actually took a marathon walk through Brooklyn, Upper Manhattan, and the Bronx on Thursday, and only returned to the yeshiva the following Monday.

Sunday—the first proper day of the shiva when we were receiving neighbors, family, and friends—was what Elissa would refer to as a "zoo," with perhaps a hundred folk passing through over the course of the day. Monday, Tuesday, and Wednesday were quieter days, with the visits starting later in the day and the visitors constituting smaller groups in different constellations from various aspects of my brother Daniel's and my respective lives. Between the young academic scholars from Orthodox backgrounds who are Daniel's advanced students, the visitors from the yeshiva (Rabbi Karp and Isaac Maxon one day, and Yisroel Ruven with Simcha Goldman the next), and the general interest in learning something about who our mother had been, I had the chance to rehearse several times the story about our "big *yichus*" (distinguished ancestry) that, in the world of traditional Torah study, both authenticates me and points out a legacy that, as I inevitably feel, I have been remiss in claiming.

That story, in a moment; but first, the most awkward, and, in hindsight, the funniest moment of the shiva. I was seated on cushions on the floor of our living room, my back against a couch on the far wall near the window, facing the door to the apartment. Simcha Goldman and Yisroel Ruven Hersh sat on either side of me, dressed in their yeshiva black suits, white shirts, and neckties, Yisroel Ruven still with his large black hat on. We were discussing at that moment, perhaps, how long Simcha had known me, since he's clearly a decade or so younger, yet it seemed to me he remembered me from my days at MTJ in the 1980s. He concurred that he remembered me, but as best we could determine together, it must have been because he was a student at MTJ in those years. While we sat together, an unmarried female friend from the Stanton Street Shul walked in. I realized she was expecting to offer me a hug, something quite improper given the strict separation of men and women that is the standard at MTJ. Here I was, flanked by dark suits and hats, with my friend approaching me with open arms and no way to escape. I frantically but as discreetly as I could—wanting neither to offend her nor to signal, any more than absolutely necessary, to Simcha and Yisroel Ruven what I was doing—moved my arms to warn her away. They said nothing, and fortunately she wasn't offended once she realized the faux pas I was trying to avoid.

A shiva is an open house, and that means a certain amount of inadvertent self-exposure. The mix of visitors was wonderful and at times unnerving; what do the visitors expect (if anything) and what do they see? I don't expect invitations to the homes of any of the people I've studied with at MTJ, though I did write about attendance at a shiva minyan on Grand Street in my last book. The Lower East Side Orthodox community tends in any case to keep its home life private rather than engaging in much casual visiting, even on the Sabbath and holidays. But a shiva changes all that.

I only received one small hint of what my shiva visitors from the yeshiva made of the people and things they saw in our home. The Rosh Yeshiva's shiur had by then (in my temporary absence) reached the eighth chapter of Gittin, which contains a brief discussion of whether a bill of divorce thrown by the husband onto a *pisla* (defined by the commentators as a kind of board) constitutes a transfer of the document sufficient to effect the divorce. That in turn depends partly on whether this board legally constitutes a separate domain, which would require that it have certain minimum dimensions—unless it is an object that is distinctively named. "Like 'that Victorian lampstand in the corner,'" I offered by way of illustrating what a "distinctively named" object would be, thinking of some of the furniture Elissa has amassed in the living room.

"No," Yisroel Ruven responded, "like those two things you have in the foyer—those two . . . lions" (about two feet tall, of hollow but heavy molded metal, which flank the armoire facing the door). So that much at least made an impression on him.

Conversation at a shiva is supposed to focus on the memory of the deceased, and where appropriate and feasible, may include recollections of her or his ancestry. Thus, it was an opportunity for me to speak of my own antecedents, the memory of whom helps give me courage to find a place in the yeshiva. I knew all this before, of course, and rehearsed it all before, but never as many times in a short period as during that shiva. "My great-grandmother Miriam, my mother's father's mother, was married to a young scholar who was a student of Reb Chaim Soloveitchik, the Brisker Rov." (Daniel says our great-grandfather was the *talmid muvhak* [favored or primary student] of Reb Chaim, an additional claim that I did not mention at the shiva.) "That scholar, her husband Reb Aharon Lebedever, died, leaving my great-grandmother a widow with one child, my grandfather Yeshaya. Around the same time the rosh yeshiva in Telz, one of the great Lithuanian yeshivas, Reb Yosef Leib Bloch, became a widower. They became remarried to each other, and my great-grandmother moved to Telz with her child, raising my grandfather together with the sons of the rosh yeshiva." Depending on who I was speaking to, I may have added, "And my grandfather came to America, because he didn't want to be a rosh yeshiva." (And my brother may have added the corrective, "He became an insurance man, but the day he retired he returned to the beis medresh.") I even added once, if I remember correctly, "And it's an ambiguous legacy. Because what's the value of this *yichus* if I don't claim it for myself?"

I was reminded of that ambiguous legacy by an encounter one winter, a few years before my kollel year. While attending a convention of the American Academy of Religion in Washington, DC, an academic Talmudist friend and I went on Shabbes morning to attend the progressive-Orthodox DC Minyan. Rabbi Shai Held, who later became the founder of the egalitarian yeshiva known as Mechon Hadar on the Upper West Side of Manhattan, happened to be presiding as gabbai. I was called to recite the blessings before and after a portion of the Torah reading, which I read, as I always do, in my best imitation of a classic Lithuanian Jewish Hebrew pronunciation. After I finished, Shai said, "You sound like a *ben torah* [someone trained in and devoted to the study and other disciplines of a Torah scholar]." I thought later: actually, a *ben bas ben toyre*, that is, the son of the daughter of a son of the Torah: my grandfather Yeshaya, that is, was the ben toyre I was striving to honor, at least with my pronunciation of these particular blessings.

This sense of a legacy that cannot be simply granted but must be taken up is part of what led me to spend time at MTJ, it seems. Yet some time after the shiva, as I stood leading the prayers at the Community Synagogue one morning (an honor frequently given to mourners), I found myself wishing I were driving aimlessly through some Rust Belt landscape, indulging the odd attraction middle-American towns that have seen better days seem to hold for me. Can't be learning at MTJ and searching for America quite at the same time, I suppose.

Ethnography Is Nonmastery

Occasionally, as mentioned above, ten- or twelve-year-old boys would be allowed to sit in the beis medresh. I watched them arguing over a Gemara, already competent at reading the text without any English "elucidation," such as that offered by the ArtScroll edition. Indeed, there's no reason to assume that the sometimes rather formal English of the ArtScroll text would be very helpful to them at that age. It somehow seemed to bring home to me that I remain and will likely for the rest of my life remain a beginner, never having gotten that competence in childhood or even young adulthood. That, in any case, was my best stab at explaining a dream I had, one Friday morning when I took an extra snooze after returning from morning services in my neighborhood. In the dream, I noticed that there were after-school Hebrew language classes at a local public school on the Lower East Side, where religious Jewish children studied separately, boys and girls.[1] I decided it would be a good idea for me to attend those classes. Returning later, I saw a room where a number of local religious adults, men and women, were gathered, again to learn something about Hebrew. I went into the room and saw a number of academics, including an old friend with whom I'd recently had some frustrating dealings, sitting around a table at the edge of the room. I joined the academics, even though I knew I wasn't invited, telling myself I belonged there anyway. They continued gossiping among themselves, until I stage-whispered, "I think these people are expecting us to address them." The dream ended there, leaving unresolved the question of whether I was supposed to be studying with the children or lecturing to the adults.

What to Call Me

Early on in our studies together, Rabbi Goldman asked me how I would like to be addressed: "Professor?" I replied that Yoynesn or Jonathan would be fine. In fact, I was almost embarrassed at the suggestion that I be addressed by an honorific in the yeshiva. This guy's teaching me, and he should call me Professor? On the contrary. Long ago in the 1980s, when I was finishing my dissertation and then when I was a new PhD with no academic position, one of the things that attracted me most about MTJ was the opportunity to participate in an intellectual, disciplined institution fully independent of the university.

So no, I didn't particularly want to be called Professor at the yeshiva, but ultimately it wasn't up to me. In late February of my kollel year, a tall young man addressed me as we were waiting for the shiur to begin: "We missed you Saturday night" (at the kollel wives' *melave malke*, the Saturday night, post-Shabbes festive meal, which Elissa did attend while I was out of town).

"My wife was there."

"I know, I talked to her. . . . Did you ever meet Michael Jordan?" (suggesting that he had learned from her that I taught at UNC, although I may have mentioned it before). At this point, the fact that I'm a professor became general knowledge in the Rosh Yeshiva's shiur.

A few days later I was taking the notes above while the Mashgiach was giving his mussar shmues, remembering how good it felt to be at that shiur, how amazing it was that all these learned people were calling me "professor," and thinking, "I'm due for a fall." At that I looked up to listen to the Mashgiach, who was talking about computer technology, which he confessed he doesn't understand well. He looked at me just as I looked up: "Professor, did I get it right?" I tried to shrug appropriately to indicate that I know nothing about computers, and at the same time to avoid seeming somehow disrespectful. I was embarrassed at the assumption that I should know about modern technology because I work in a secular institution, and also embarrassed that in fact I don't.

Later, I approached him with a story that, I hoped, would resonate with our shared innocence of computer technology. The joke is included in an early chapter of Uriel Weinreich's textbook *College Yiddish*:

Two Jews are talking about the new telegraph. One says, "I don't understand how it works."

The other says, "Imagine a giant dog, with its tail in Vilna and its head in Kovno. You pull the tail in Vilna, and it barks in Kovno."

"Yeah, but how does the telegraph work?"

"The same way, but without the dog."

In return, the Mashgiach told me: "My grandfather came from a shtetl called Horodets. He remembered when they first put a mailbox there. People didn't understand how it worked: You put a letter in it, and a few weeks later a letter comes back to you. They figured, probably there's a little *mentshele* [a tiny person] inside the box.[2] How does the mentshele know where the letter's supposed to go? So when you drop the letter in, *shray arayn*, shout into it the address where the letter's supposed to go. And when I was a kid, when my father would ask me to mail a letter, he'd always remind me: '*Shray arayn!*'"

Five Times Rabbi

Twice on the same day in February 2012, I was given the message that I "should" become a rabbi, and as it had happened on at least three occasions before that as well, I decided to record all these messages, as follows:

- A few years ago a Christian gentleman who somehow honored Jews and our synagogue enough to volunteer to clean up at Stanton Street every Friday afternoon in preparation for the Sabbath, spoke to me in the vestibule: "I know you're a professor and you're not a rabbi, but you really should think of becoming one."
- In October 2011, on a brief visit to Vanderbilt University, I took a long evening walk to Nashville's honky-tonk strip. As I stood outside one of the bars where the singer was belting, "Why-y-y do I drink?" and the audience responded in unison, "To get drunk!" a young man staggered out, gave me a high five, and declared, "I drank too much!" He followed me down the block, and seeing my black velvet yarmulke, eventually slurred, "Are you a rabbi?" I told him I wasn't, but he insisted, "Well, you should study and become one!"
- In the weeks before my kollel year, a few weeks after the initial conversation with Rabbi Brody in which he suggested I attend the Rosh Yeshiva's shiur, he added: "Here's a crazy thought: Why not really attend MTJ full time and see if you can get smicha at the end of it? There's a big corporate lawyer named——. His father is a rabbi at a yeshiva in England, and the son always thought his father was disappointed that he never became a rabbi. So he took a year off, went to all of the shiurim, and by the end of the year he got smicha."
- One day Max Greenberg, who was then still studying for religious ordination himself, said, "You're becoming a regular—maybe you should get smicha here!" I told him my wife would divorce me if I became a rabbi, and he said, "Why, because then she'd have to ask you all her *shayles*?"
- And on the same day, as I made my way out of the yeshiva, Effi, the Rosh Yeshiva's assistant, said to me, "Rabbi, where do you daven?" Effi and I have known each other a long time already, since he runs the Chasam Sopher Shul around

the corner from Stanton Street. But I didn't remember him ever calling me "rabbi" before.

In any case, I wasn't thinking that far ahead yet, unless it was to hope somehow this narrative didn't turn into a story about how I became a rabbi. Not that there seemed much risk of that. At a certain point in my ArtScroll review I had just completed the tractate Beitzah, about the laws particular to holy days. So in my solo study time at the yeshiva I decided to take a look at the volume known as the *Yam shel Shlomo*, by the sixteenth-century scholar Solomon Luria, known as the Maharshal. I figured it would be good practice for me to consult a secondary text, in the original language, on something—anything—relating to the topic I'd just been studying in ArtScroll. My first attempt to work through one of his halachic essays—which is completely unpunctuated, printed in the particular typeface known as "Rashi script,"[3] and full of abbreviations that continue to baffle me despite Simcha Goldman's best efforts to make me a more fluent reader of this type of text—left me with the somewhat uncomfortable sense that this moment in my learning was better understood as a pure meditative practice than as self-instruction. That's not necessarily a bad thing. Yet it was hard for me not to feel that, at age fifty-five, I had an awful lot of catching up to do; and such anxiety is not, I think, the beginning of wisdom.

How Are Others Called?

At the beginning, Yisroel Ruven was perhaps the most clued in to the potentially threatening possibility that I might write a book about the yeshiva. One day a thirteen-year-old youngster whom I didn't know visited the Rosh Yeshiva's shiur, and Yisroel Ruven chatted him up beforehand: "And if anybody calls me 'rabbi,' it's a lie." Then Yisroel Ruven turned to me: "There, I just gave you something." I never quite figured out what it was that he had given me, though at the time, the fact that he wasn't a rabbi was indeed news to me. I noted shortly afterwards that I'd never heard him called Rabbi Hersh. Perhaps not acquiring ordination is, for him, a mark of his devotion to study for its own sake.

So "they" are not all rabbis. On the other hand, I'm not the only "professor." For some reason it took me a long time to learn the name, and even the hometown, of one of the shiur regulars, whom I've called Rabbi Pinsker here. My first notes call him "Teaneck," but actually he lives in Passaic, a slightly less expensive, and for the most part somewhat more traditionally Orthodox, suburban Jewish community. He teaches computing for accountants at Baruch College, one of the City University of New York campuses. One day when his usual study partner was out, he turned to me: "Professor, would you like to prepare the Gemara for tomorrow with me?" I couldn't because I was about to study with Rabbi Karp and Rabbi Weiss. I told him in any case to please call me Jonathan, but he said he wouldn't remember the name. I explained further: "Out there, I'm a professor, but in here I'm just a beginner."

He replied: "Yeah, it's like that for me at Baruch [College]. There they call me 'rabbi,' but here . . ." He didn't finish the sentence. In fact, he, too, is often addressed as "professor" at MTJ—and as far as Gemara goes, I'll never catch up to him. Still, his kind reply suggested that while he may look like a rabbi in the secular world, he doesn't pretend to any special competence within the confines of MTJ.

Running Down and Charging Up

Finishing my study with Rabbi Karp around 3:10 p.m. one afternoon, I surprised myself a bit by staying on to investigate a question about the daily prayer of Tachanun (supplication). The prayer begins with a quote: "And David said let us fall into the hands of God, and into the hand of man I will not fall." Yet as these words are said, the custom is, while sitting or leaning, to rest one's forehead on one's forearm. This has always struck me as odd: You're "falling" into your own hand and saying, "I will not fall into a human hand"? Rabbi Goldman had heard my question the day before but didn't have time to study with me yesterday, so just said, "Look at the *Tur*." I looked at the *Tur* and I looked at the *Shulchan aruch*, and what I read there confused me further. According to them, this prayer is optional, not obligatory. They do say that if you prostrate yourself at the beginning of Tachanun, you shouldn't stretch out your hands and feet (because that appears like idolatry); actually, you should "lean" on one side. Moreover, the text in *Tur* appears entirely different (and much shorter, as far as I can tell) than the one we use. So what I established from that brief review is, at least tentatively, that our practice cannot be derived directly from these decisors.

As a result, I was still in the beis medresh at 4:00 p.m., when Rabbi Karp finished studying with Isaac Maxon, and to my surprise he asked me if I wanted to continue our study of the tractate Arachin. Which we did, until 5:30 p.m., and it was gratifying and exhausting to have that extra time with him. I gradually developed a headache—perhaps from so much squinting at small letters, but perhaps also because there was dust in our apartment from a kitchen remodeling job, still barely begun—that I hadn't quite shaken the next morning, when I recorded these quotidian goings-on at the beis medresh.

Ideally, of course, and often in fact, the study is exhilarating as well. In mid-January of 2014, I took my leave, as my semester in Ithaca was about to begin. Rabbi Karp said: "You got charged up for the zman [term]. And you know how to do it!" It was both a creative and a generous statement. Usually, "to get charged up for the zman" refers to recreational periods in between set calendar times for full-time yeshiva study. Here, he made a double substitution: "getting charged up" referred instead to my choice to spend my break from my academic calendar in the yeshiva, while he dignified my academic semester with the yeshiva term "zman."

Permission to Publish

Through the following two academic years after my kollel year, and especially as I continued to come to the yeshiva when I could, and, from time to time, take notes, I became more and more confident that there was indeed a book hidden in those notes. One day while crossing the Arts Quad at Cornell I realized: "But I'll have to ask the Rosh Yeshiva's permission first."

It took me a few more months to gather the courage, and then another few weeks to find the opportunity. How was I to broach this question with a man whose authority was unquestioned and to whom, although I had sat in his shiur for a few years, I had barely said more than "Good Shabbes"? I practiced my explanation in my head. When I rehearsed it to friend who's an academic Talmudist over dinner in Ithaca one evening, he said, "You got me when you told me it has to do with your *parnosse* [livelihood]."

To be sure, I had plenty of clues that what it takes to earn an honest living played a considerable role in a number of the Rosh Yeshiva's dicta, and of his father's rulings as well. One day in May 2014, I missed a siyum celebrating the group's completion of a chapter in the Gemara. Asher filled me in one some of the good lines I'd missed: "I finally asked him a question I'd been embarrassed to ask for far too long. What about paintball? Is it *mutar* [permitted] or *osur* [forbidden]? And he said that since there's a risk that you'll get bloodied or bruised, and there's no other benefit from it, it's osur. Once someone asked him about a *shomer shabbes* [Sabbath-observant] boxer, and he said, 'Well, he's doing it for a living.' As to baseball, he says the kids are used to doing it already, and they get their excess energy out that way [so there's a benefit to it]." So I knew it was important to explain how publishing a book about the yeshiva was linked to how I earn my living.

My notes from December 17, 2014, read: "Rebbi comes in and my heart races, because after shiur, I'm planning to ask his permission to write a book about the beis medresh." But I didn't get to ask him that day, and had to wait almost a week. Here's what

I wrote about the day I finally got to ask him for permission to write a book about MTJ:

December 23, 2014: A young couple from Lakewood with a baby are waiting with me; they have an appointment with the Rosh Yeshiva for 12:30. I try to make the baby smile without inappropriately looking at the woman.

Right now I'm be[tting he'll say no; I didn't get to finish writing that sentence because the young couple came out and I had my chance to go in.]

I stand for a moment by the open door, waiting for him to finish perusing a document, sign it, and look up. I begin the speech I've rehearsed many times by now, sometimes to myself and sometimes live (to several younger colleagues, I think also to Nasanel): "Maybe the Rebbi knows that I spent a couple of years learning here in the '80s. It's been a great privilege and pleasure to be able to spend time learning here the last few years. Of course I have to work most of the time, but I'm fortunate to have a job that gives me a lot of free time. I had a leave from work coming up in 2012, and Rabbi Brody suggested, 'Why don't you go to the Rosh Yeshivah's shiur?' I've been very happy, and I hope to keep learning here for many years.

"I think the Rebbi knows that I teach and write about Jewish communities for a living. I wrote my dissertation, a book about Polish Jews in Paris, and I've written a book about my shul here on the Lower East Side. Now I would very much like to write a book about the beis medresh."

The Rebbi replied, "Why not?"

Well, in my many imaginings of this conversation, that was one response I thought he might possibly make. I went on to promise to disguise as much as I could, although I had to admit I wouldn't be able to disguise the place itself, because it's unique.

"That's a good idea," he responded. "That way you'll have the *ruchniyes* [the spirit] without the *gashmiyes* [the matter]."

Yet he had one more question: "I don't understand what it has to do with parnosse." So I explained: it's certainly not because you make money from the books. Rather, you write a dissertation to get a PhD. If you're lucky, you get a job. You write a book to get tenure, and another to become a full professor. Quickly I went on to explain that at my stage, I wouldn't lose my job if I didn't publish another book, but it's an expected part of doing the job in an honorable fashion.

He shook my hand with the Yiddish words, "Zol zayn mit hatslokhe" (may your venture be successful). I guess it isn't as big a deal to him as it is to me, but as I had started writing before I went into his office, I had myself thinking he certainly would say no. And if he had, that would have been an end to it. In this respect, to be sure, he is my Rebbi.

I walked back across the hall into the beis medresh, clapped Nasanel on the back, and quoted, "'Why not?'"

Nasanel replied, "Mazel tov!"

A few weeks later, I went off to California to spend a long weekend with our son Jonah. I was just then working through the last volume of the ArtScroll tractate Bava Basra (the longest tractate in the Babylonian Talmud). I didn't want to carry the heavy volume on the plane, so I raced through it before I left. My mother's *yortsayt* (the anniversary of her death) was the day before I was to leave, and that, combined with the sense of a "zman" (my winter break from teaching in Ithaca) ending for me, inspired me to mark the completion of Bava Basra with a siyum—something I don't frequently do, partly because others rarely seem to make a siyum on their own study, and partly because I'm taking massive shortcuts by using the ArtScroll to begin with. But Rabbi Goldman and Rabbi Karp seem to enjoy it when I make a siyum.

The very end of Bava Basra deals with the question of whether and under what circumstances someone who offers to guarantee a third party's loan will be held to that offer (or, by contrast, under what circumstances it is considered merely a nonbinding way to encourage the loan). The conclusion is that if the offer is made before a rabbinical court, it is binding, because of the *hanoye* (benefit) the guarantor gets from being recognized by the court. I summarized this in my siyum, and then concluded, "In consideration of the profound hanoye I have gotten from being accepted into this community of scholars, I pledge myself to be a guarantor of the good name and healthy functioning of this beis medresh for many years to come."

7

Learning and the Time
of the Dream

FROM MY NOTEBOOK:

March 2, 2012: A dream just before waking: It's 3:00 p.m. on a Friday (today is Friday morning), and all of the teachers and boys from MTJ's lower school are gathered in a room that looks like something between the beis medresh and the cafeteria. One of the teachers is in the front of the room, and it seems that the meeting is about planning a Purim party. However, as he speaks he begins to leap about the room, clowning as one might on Purim. Returning to the front of the room, he continues to cut up, lift his pants leg a bit and dance, making all of the kids laugh. I sense myself beginning to weep for all of the dead Jewish children and wake up, my throat sore from the reflux that's returned in recent months and that I have neglected to treat properly.

In this dream I seem to wish to merge young Orthodox American boys today not only with those Jewish children murdered by the Nazis and their local henchmen, but perhaps as well with the fragmented memories of an imagined, more whole or "authentic" Jewish childhood in eastern Europe. The impulse to repair the breach of memory—and perhaps my ambivalence about that impulse—is certainly part of my impulse for studying at MTJ, as it has directed my professional life for the past four decades.

Another dream was about my mother's father, Yeshaya Kravits, who somehow became Cyrus Weltman in America. In this dream we—but I don't remember exactly who—were bringing him home to live with us. He was younger in the dream than I remember him in life. In the dream, I spoke with him briefly. He spoke coherently in full sentences, but not about anything that is pertinent to what I would want to learn from him. In life, as I had told Nasanel, he had spent his last few years institutionalized with Alzheimer's. Relating the dream to Elissa later that morning, I told her it makes me understand people's impulse to want to be reunited with their families in heaven: I imagine learning with him in Yiddish as the greatest pleasure possible.

At yeshiva, waiting for shiur to start, I began to tell Nasanel about the dream, getting as far as explaining that my grandfather had in fact been institutionalized and that I dreamed we took him home. He wouldn't let me get to the second part, about my waking and longing to learn with my grandfather. He did say, however, that according to the Gemara (except for the minority view of Rabbi Meir) (Gittin 52a), the dream has a meaning that we are bound to try to understand. Knowing what he does about my family, he suggested that it meant we should bring our disabled son, Yeshaya, the namesake of my grandfather, home to live with us. Rather than having me relate the rest of the dream, he said it would be better for me to forget the whole thing because with the prevailing conceptions of my "social milieu" (one of his favorite terms, which he uses to tease me for my cultural relativist mindset), I'm not in a position to take it seriously enough "even though you also have some shtetl mystical sentimentalism as well."

The next day, I did get to tell Nasanel the "end" of my dream, about the desire to study with my grandfather. He decided to mollify me somewhat: "I realize that you are who you are, and so the suggestion that you have your son home with you with a twenty-four-hour aide is not realistic in your situation. But you should name your grandchild after your grandfather." Then I told him that our son's name is actually Yeshaya, which he hadn't known yesterday. "Of course I didn't know that, that's how dreams work, they sputter forth."

The next Sunday afternoon I went to Brooklyn to visit our son Yeshaya. I told Nasanel that I would be going there—both because I knew of his expressed concern for our son not living with us, and because in the morning when we were planning when we would study together, he'd suggested, half-seriously, that he should arrange to study with me later rather than earlier to ensure that I stayed at the beis medresh longer. If he weren't so intelligent and sincere I would find this really annoying. After I came back and studied for a while, I got up to go home, but Nasanel wanted to talk to me in the hall. He had spent time as a chaplain in nursing homes, and was still distressed at the neglect he had seen, even in the better ones, so he wanted to express his concerns to me, "even though I know it upsets you."

Dreams often seem to afford almost infinite time for exploration, and perhaps one of Nasanel's remarkable gifts is the ability to extend time, or to defy the shackles of quantified, linear time. This comes through, for example, in his way of making the old new, as when he was talking to me about the biblical story of Hannah and Peninah, and called them Grace and Pearl, or his habit of referring to the medieval commentator and decisor Rabbenu Tam as "Rabbi Perfect." All of these are in truth just literal translations of the Hebrew names, but somehow the English versions, rather than stripping them of Jewish particularity, here bring them closer to our own world and time.

In the waking world we are either here or there, or someplace in between. Writing the date in my notebook toward the end of one winter break, I thought of the days I had available to learn Torah slipping away. . . . I was reminded of a story I read many years ago, about Anschel Rothschild, the founder of the family banking house. It's said that when he was busy in his office, he would hire an old Jewish scholar to sit in an anteroom and learn, only interrupting his studies to come out once an hour into the office and say, "It's 1:00, Reb Anschel . . . It's 2:00, Reb Anschel."

I've always understood from that anecdote that Anschel Rothschild meant thereby to remind himself that, no matter how much wealth he might be accumulating, every hour he spent in his office was an hour lost to Torah. Rabbi Weiss gently conveyed a similar message to me, when he learned that my kollel year was about up and I was planning to return to North Carolina to resume my university teaching. A few times toward the end of December he looked at me and said, a bit sadly, "Not much time, Professor!" (until you have to leave us). And he repeated, as he's said many times over the year, "You should get a job in New York. You should stay with us."

Our table is near the big window, and Yisroel Ruven got up to shut it properly. "It got so cold all of a sudden," somebody said. I said that I like the cold—I'm worried about global warming and the cold reassures me. "Well," Yisroel Ruven said, "you're from Minneapolis . . . Cincinnati . . . someplace like that, right?"

I didn't even realize he was talking to me at first, but when I did I corrected him: "North Carolina."

"That's why you're worried, you'll get flooded there."

Rabbi Weiss, sitting next to us thought not really joining us in the preparation for the shiur, quietly said, "See, I told you you should stay in New York."

I never got even that kind of gentle pressure from Asher Stoler. Instead, when I got up to say goodbye to everyone for the time being and "bemoan" that I had to go to work, Asher said, "The truth is, for somebody who works, you probably spend more time in the beis medresh than anybody else."

Still, I felt the impending loss and somehow I wanted a blessing before I left. I mentioned to Rabbi Cantor that I'd like to speak to him after minchah. I had to wait around—a bit impatiently, forcing myself to discipline my stomach—for about twenty minutes before going down to lunch, because I hadn't realized how slowly and intently Rabbi Cantor prays. I asked him (as I had asked the

Mashgiach) to have me in mind while I'm away—that I should continue to learn, and that my intentions in learning should improve. He took my request very seriously, first asking for my Hebrew name, and that of my father and mother. "Any time you're praying for something, not just when you're sick, you should use the mother's name. I learned it from a *posuk* [scriptural verse], and I told Reb Moshe, and he liked it very much. 'Your servant the son of your maidservant' [Psalm 116:16]." Then he took my hand in his, looked intently into my eyes, and blessed me (as he had almost a year earlier) that "Hashem should make you the biggest talmid chacham that He wants you to become." The first time it sounded a bit overly pious to me. This time it sounded like a pure gift, the most heartfelt blessing I have ever received, an almost unbearably intimate moment.

How honest was I when I told Nasanel that my dream of retirement was to sit in the yeshiva full time, and not to enjoy the aesthetic pleasures that a secular academic might look forward to as his reward? Indeed, sometimes when I'm in New York and spending my time at the yeshiva, I find myself missing the college town where I happen to teach, now Ithaca. When I'm *here* I miss *there*, wherever "here" and "there" happen to be at the time. There's always an element of longing for something I don't have at the moment, a longing, it seems, that is not to be resolved in this life.

Meanwhile I am often in between. One night in early December 2014 I finished my last duty in Ithaca for the semester, a dinner for a job candidate. I had originally been planning to drive to New York the following day, but the weather in between NYC and Ithaca the next morning sounded so awful that I got in the car and drove back at night, arriving at almost 2:00 a.m. I usually avoid driving that late at night, but I just told myself that driving—and concentrating on it—was what I was going to do for the next few hours. For more than half the trip, until I'd made it past Scranton, I didn't even turn on the radio. An odometer, along with knowing how many miles I have to drive, helps the hours go by, minute by minute: a mile doesn't take so long and it's measurable. The trick is not to fall into a trance.

I thought of the trip both because it made it possible for me to be in yeshiva in time for preparation and shiur the next day, and because that kind of relaxed focus—hard enough to achieve at any time, but necessary for safe driving especially at night—struck me as analogous to the kind of concentration needed for learning well. Yet during shiur the next morning, I dozed off and saw nighttime highway before my eyes.

GLOSSARY

Acharonim: Literally "last ones"; rabbinic authorities roughly from the sixteenth century to the present.

Aguda: Agudath Israel, an organization of Orthodox Jews that represents their social and political interests in the larger public sphere.

Agunah: "Grass widow"; a woman who cannot remarry because her husband refuses to grant her a Jewish bill of divorce, or *get*, or because her husband's death has not been legally established.

Aliyah: Literally "ascent"; here, summons to step up to the reading platform and recite the blessings over a portion of the Torah reading.

Am segula: Commonly glossed as "chosen people," but more closely meaning "treasured" or "protected" people.

Amoraim: The rabbinic masters whose dicta are recorded in the Talmud and other literature of the same period.

Apikoros: a heretic.

Aruch hashulchan: Comprehensive restatement and discussion of Jewish law, written by Rabbi Yechiel Michel Epstein of Navaredok (1829–1908).

Asmachta: Proof text; a scriptural verse chosen to support a given interpretation but not its direct source.

Baal betochen: Optimist or person of straightforward religious faith.

***Baal hamaor*:** Book written by Zerachiah ben Isaac ha-Levi Gerondi (around 1125—after 1186).

Baal koyre: One who reads to the congregation from the Torah scroll.

Baal teshuva: Penitent or "returnee" to religious observance.

Bava Basra: Talmudic tractate dealing primarily with property law.

Bava Kama: Talmudic tractate dealing primarily with tort law.

Bava Metsiya: Talmudic tractate dealing with torts and property law.

***Bayis chadash* or *Bach*:** Commentary on the *Tur* by Rabbi Joel Sirkis (1561–1640).

Beis din: Rabbinic court.

Beis medresh: Study hall.

***Beis Yosef*:** Commentary to the *Tur* by Rabbi Joseph Karo, author of *Shulchan aruch*.

Beitzah: Talmudic tractate dealing with laws pertaining to Jewish holidays.

Bimah: Lectern for public recitation of the Torah.

Bokhurim: Unmarried yeshiva students.

Chalitzah: Ritual of refusal of levirate marriage (see *yibum*).

Chazon ish: Magnum opus of Rabbi Avraham Yeshaya Karelitz (1878–1953).

Chofetz chaim: Ethical treatise by Rabbi Yisrael Meir Kagan (1838–1933).

Cholov yisroel: Literally "Jewish milk"; dairy products made from milk that has been milked under the supervision of a religiously observant Jew.

Chomets: Leavened food products, forbidden on Passover.

Chumrah: Stringent ruling.

Daas Torah: The views of leading religious figures in a given generation on various matters, including but not limited to religious law.

Daf yomi: Literally "folio of the day," referring to the worldwide program whose participants study the same folio of the Babylonian Talmud.

Davening for the amud: Leading the congregation in prayer.

Elul: The Hebrew month prior to Rosh Hashanah, at the beginning of autumn.

Elul zman: The term of study beginning with the month of Elul.

Farbisn: Here, bitter.

Farfrumt: Overly pious or excessively stringent in religious practice.

Frum: Literally "pious," but generally meaning a religiously observant Jew.

Gabbai: Here, secretary or assistant who helps manage the schedule of the Rosh Yeshiva.

Gashmiyes: Materiality.

Gedolim: Leading rabbinic figures of a given generation.

Gemara: Text of the Talmud.

Gittin: Talmudic tractate dealing with divorce law.

Goles: Exile.

Goy: Non-Jew.

Halacha: Jewish law.

Halacha lemoshe misinai: Law dictated to Moses at Mt. Sinai but not recorded in Scripture.

Hasofah: Extra aliyah.

Hava amina: Literally "I would have thought"; a potentially different interpretation.

Kaddish: Memorial prayer for the dead.

Karo, Rabbi Joseph: Jewish mystic and halachic authority; author of the *Shulchan aruch* and the *Beis Yosef.*

Kedusha: Literally "sanctity"; prayer recited by the leader of the congregation, focusing on the holiness of the Divinity.

Kheyder: Traditional religious school for young children.

Khsides: Hasidism.

Khumesh: The Five Books of Moses.

Kinyan: Performance of legal acquisition.

Kollel: Institution where (often recently) married men continue intensive study.

Kotsk (Kotsker Rebbe): Rabbi Menachem Mendl Morgenstern (1787–1859), a leading figure in Polish Hasidism.

Layen: To read from the Torah in public (see *baal koyre*).

Lehavdil: Term used to introduce a distinction between two items being compared.

Levaye: Funeral.

Loshen hora: Derogatory gossip.

Loshen koydesh: The Holy Tongue; Hebrew-Aramaic.

Maharsha: Rabbi Samuel Eidels (1555–1631), whose commentaries are often helpful in resolving particularly thorny issues in Talmud interpretation.

Masechet Sofrim: One of the "minor tractates," dated later and printed as an addendum to the Babylonian Talmud, dealing largely with rules for Hebrew scribes and the recitation of Scripture.

Mashgiach: Shortened version of *mashgiach ruchani*, or spiritual supervisor, responsible for the moral training of yeshiva students.

Maskil: Enlightener; participant in or follower of the Haskalah or "Jewish Enlightenment," hence a nonbeliever.

Mechitzah: Partition, here meaning a physical separation between men's and women's sections.

Mezuzah: Literally "doorpost"; container into which are placed certain scriptural passages, affixed to the doorpost of rooms in a Jewish home or institution.

Minchah: Afternoon prayer.

Minhag: Custom.

Mishnah: Authoritative collection of rabbinic rulings and sayings, generally dated to the second century CE.

Mishnah berurah: Authoritative commentary on *Orach chaim*, the section of the *Shulchan aruch* covering behavior in daily Jewish life, by Rabbi Yisrael Meir Kagan (Poland, 1838–1933), also known as the Chofetz Chaim.

Mussar: Moral education or exhortation.

Mussar shmues: A lesson in mussar, frequently part of the regular curriculum of Lithuanian-style yeshivas.

Ne'eman: Trustworthy person or trustee.

Olam hazeh: This world.

Parnosse: Livelihood.

Pasken: To issue a halachic ruling.

Posek: Religious decisor.

Posuk: Verse.

Pshat: Plain meaning.

Pushkes: Collection boxes.

Rabosay: "Gentlemen" (often used to open an address to a group).

Rambam: Rabbi Moshe ben Maimon, or Maimonides (1135–1204).

Ran: Rabbi Nissim ben Reuven of Gerona (1320–1376).

Rashash: Samuel Strashun of Vilna (1794–1872).

Rashba: Rabbi Solomon ben Avraham of Barcelona (1235–1310).

Rashi: Rabbi Solomon Yitzhaki (1040–1105), author of the most comprehensive and authoritative commentaries on the Bible and Talmud.

Refues: Cures.

Rif: Rabbi Isaac Alfasi (1013–1103).

Rishon: One of the "first ones," leading rabbinic authorities from the eleventh to the fifteenth century.

Rosh: Head (as a body part, and also as a leader).

Ruchniyes: Spirituality.

Sefer: Religious book.

Segules: Amulets.

Shach: Commentary on the *Shulchan aruch* by Rabbi Shabbatai ben Meir HaKohen (1621–1662).

Shales sudes: The ritual "third meal" late on Sabbath afternoon.

Shayle: Question, commonly concerning correct practice.

Shemets: Hint or trace.

Sheva brokhes: The seven blessings recited at a Jewish wedding ceremony; hence, one of the cycle of ritual feasts in the days immediately following a Jewish wedding, after each of which the blessings are again recited.

Shiva: Seven-day mourning period for a close relative.

Shulchan aruch: The authoritative code of Jewish law written by Joseph Karo, first published in 1563.

Shviger: Mother-in-law.

Siddur: Prayer book.

Siyum: Completion of a unit of study; hence, the celebration of that accomplishment.

Soncino (here, Talmud): An English translation of the Babylonian Talmud from the first half of the twentieth century.

Sotah: Woman suspected of adultery.

Tachanun: Penitential prayers recited as part of the morning and afternoon daily services.

Talmidim: Students or disciples.

Talmud: Here, generally the Babylonian Talmud; an extensive set of texts structured as commentary and elaboration on the Mishnah, first compiled in late antiquity.

Tannaim: The rabbis whose dicta are recorded in the Mishnah.

Taz: Rabbi David Halevi (1586–1667), so called after his commentary *Turei zahav* (pillars of gold) on the *Shulchan aruch*.

Tefillin: Leather boxes containing certain scriptural passages, attached to the top of the head and to the arm with leather straps, and worn during morning prayers.

Teshuva: Here, a written response to a question in rabbinic law.

Tosafos: A group of authoritative Talmud commentators in the generations after Rashi.

Tur: Jewish legal code composed by Jacob ben Asher (1270–1340), whose organization of topics was followed by the later *Shulchan aruch*.

Tzaddik: Saint or extraordinarily pious individual.

Yam shel Shlomo: "Solomon's sea," the most prominent work of Rabbi Solomon Luria (1510–1573).

Yibum: The levirate marriage; scriptural requirement for a brother to marry the wife of a brother who died childless.

Yortsayt: Anniversary of someone's death.

Zichus: Accumulated merit.

Zman: Term as part of an academic year.

NOTES

Preface

1. See my "Voices around the Text: The Ethnography of Reading at Mesivta Tifereth Jerusalem," *Cultural Anthropology* 4, no. 4 (November 1993): 399–421.

Chapter One

1. Agudath Israel, founded in Europe in the early twentieth century, remains a strong force linking various segments of the traditional Orthodox Jewish world.

2. This, it seems, can't be right, since the issue came up some time later and Yisroel Ruven insisted then that, quite on the contrary and following the ruling of Reb Moshe Feinstein, he will eat any dairy product that has a reliable kashrut certificate.

3. See Menachem Friedman, "The 'Family-Community' Model in Haredi Society," in *Coping with Life and Death: The Jewish Family in the Twentieth Century*, Studies in Contemporary Jewry 14, ed. Peter Y. Medding (New York: Oxford University Press, 1998), 166–77.

4. Audra Simpson, "On Ethnographic Refusal: Indigeneity, 'Voice,' and Colonial Citizenship," *Junctures: The Journal for Thematic Dialogue* 9 (2007): 67–80.

Chapter Two

1. As I realized years later, this vociferous scholar must have been studying the talmudic tractate Sukkah (at folio 26b). The question, "How long does a horse sleep?," which I took to be the speaker's own, is in fact asked in the text of the Gemara itself.

2. Literally "page of the day," this phrase refers to the practice of studying a page of the Babylonian Talmud each day, on a schedule coordinated with thousands of other readers around the world. The entire cycle takes just under seven and a half years.

3. Placed in bold because it somehow seems to echo or speak to my sense, from almost the beginning of my "fieldwork" at MTJ, that there's a "last of the Mohicans" feeling about the place and people are aware of it.

4. Clearly, "stuff" and the Yiddish "shtup" are cognates.

Chapter Three

1. Babylonian Talmud Taanit 22b: "Do not count on miracles. And even if you find a way to say that a miracle will be performed for [you,] it will be deducted from [your] merits."

2. I referred earlier to Braslaver Hasidim as "the guys with long hair and the multicolored clothes." That group of followers of the long-deceased Reb Nachman of Braslav has grown rapidly over the past few decades. However, the three young men referred to here are members of the older, more traditionalist community of Braslaver Hasidim based in Brooklyn.

3. That building was heavily damaged by fire on May 14, 2017, and the Landmarks Preservation Commission approved an application for a demolition permit in July of that year.

4. I didn't know what the salmon issue was, until the Internet told me it had to do with worm infestation.

5. Another bug issue, this one about microscopic crustaceans in New York City tap water; I knew about this from neighborhood hearsay rather than anything I'd heard recently in the yeshiva.

6. Two modern halachic codes, both by nonhasidic "Lithuanian" rabbis.

7. Isaac ben Judah Abarbanel (1437–1508), of Portugal.

8. Reb Nasanel ben Asher, author of the *Arba Turim* or "Tur," discussed in chapter 4.

Chapter Four

1. The creation of something called Orthodox Judaism is a complex matter, but suffice it here to say that no one had heard of such a thing until nineteenth-century Reformers attacked what *they* designated as "Orthodoxy."

2. This last bit reminds me of a story my teacher Shlomo Noble told me when I was collecting his memoirs in the early 1980s. When the Schiff Classics edition of Psalms was being prepared, there was a line in the English translation: "the maker in his infinite wisdom." Since "maker" here refers to God, the proofreader wanted a capital "M," and wrote next to the word: "CAP." So the line was printed, "The capmaker in his infinite wisdom."

Chapter Five

1. For a historical perspective on breaks and continuities in Orthodox tradition, see the classic article by Haym Soloveitchik, "Rupture and Reconstruction: The Transformation of Contemporary Orthodoxy," *Tradition* 28, no. 4 (Summer 1994): 64–130.

Chapter Six

1. "Simulated Shiur: Post-It Notes of an ArtScroll Amateur," in *Jewish Rhetoric: History, Culture, Theory*, ed. Michael Bernard-Donals and Jan Fernheimer (Hanover, NH: Brandeis University Press, 2014), 215–30.

2. "Observant Participation: The Ethnography of Jews on the Lower East Side," *YIVO Annual of Jewish Social Science* (1990): 233–54.

Chapter Seven

1. A source for this much of the dream: As part of our kitchen renovation work in 2012, Elissa went to Borough Park to shop for appliances at a store called A. J. Madison, on Thirty-Eighth Street. Passing a playground she had known as a child, she noticed (and reported to me, and then several more times to others in my hearing) that while it remains a public park, it now has a fence down the middle, and separate entrances where boys and girls go in. She reports that it's near the Sanzer hasidic yeshiva, and suspects that it's mostly used by children who go there.

2. For me, inevitably raising Walter Benjamin's image of the chess-playing automaton that Benjamin likens to the Angel of History.

3. Not because Rashi wrote in that script, but because Rashi's commentary is printed in that font.

INDEX

A NOTE ON THE TYPE

This book has been composed in Arno, an Old-style serif typeface in the
classic Venetian tradition, designed by Robert Slimbach at Adobe.

Lightning Source UK Ltd.
Milton Keynes UK
UKHW011313161020
371706UK00002B/171